MAJOR
PRESIDENTIAL
ELECTIONS
and the administrations that followed
The Election of
1828
and the Administration of
Andrew Jackson
EDITOR
Arthur M. Schlesinger jr.
ASSOCIATE EDITORS
Fred L. Israel & David J. Frent

The Elections of 1789 & 1792 and the Administration of George Washington

The Election of 1800 and the Administration of Thomas Jefferson

The Election of 1828 and the Administration of Andrew Jackson

The Election of 1840 and the Harrison/Tyler Administrations

The Election of 1860 and the Administration of Abraham Lincoln

The Election of 1876 and the Administration of Rutherford B. Hayes

The Election of 1896 and the Administration of William McKinley

The Election of 1912 and the Administration of Woodrow Wilson

The Election of 1932 and the Administration of Franklin D. Roosevelt

The Election of 1948 and the Administration of Harry S. Truman

The Election of 1960 and the Administration of John F. Kennedy

The Election of 1968 and the Administration of Richard Nixon

The Election of 1976 and the Administration of Jimmy Carter

The Election of 1980 and the Administration of Ronald Reagan

The Election of 2000 and the Administration of George W. Bush

The Election of 1828

and the Administration of Andrew Jackson

EDITOR

Arthur M. Schlesinger, jr.
Albert Schweitzer Chair in the Humanities
The City University of New York

ASSOCIATE EDITORS

Fred L. Israel
Department of History
The City College of New York

David J. Frent
The David J. and Janice L. Frent
Political Americana Collection

Mason Crest Publishers
Philadelphia

Produced by OTTN Publishing, Stockton, New Jersey

Mason Crest Publishers
370 Reed Road
Broomall PA 19008
www.masoncrest.com

Contributing Editor: Christopher Higgins
Research Consultant: Patrick K. Hilferty
Editorial Assistant: Jane Ziff

First printing

1 3 5 7 9 8 6 4 2

Library of Congress Cataloging-in-Publication Data

The election of 1828 / editor Arthur M. Schlesinger Jr.; associate editors Fred L. Israel & David J. Frent.
p. cm. — (Major presidential elections and the administrations that followed)
Summary: Discusses the presidential election of 1828 and the subsequent administration of Andrew Jackson.
Includes bibliographical references and index.
ISBN 1-59084-353-3
1. United States—Politics and government—1829-1837—Sources. 2. United States—Politics and government—1825-1829—Sources. 3. United States—History—1815-1861—Sources. 4. Presidents—United States—Election—1828—Juvenile literature. [1. Presidents—Election—1828. 2. Elections. 3. Jackson, Andrew, 1767-1845. 4. United States—Politics and government—1829-1837. 5. United States—Politics and government—1825-1829.]
I. Schlesinger, Arthur Meier, 1917- II. Israel, Fred L. III. Frent, David J. IV. Series.
E381 .E45 2003
324.973'055—dc21

2002071802

Publisher's note: all quotations in this book come from original sources, and contain the spelling and grammatical inconsistencies of the original text.

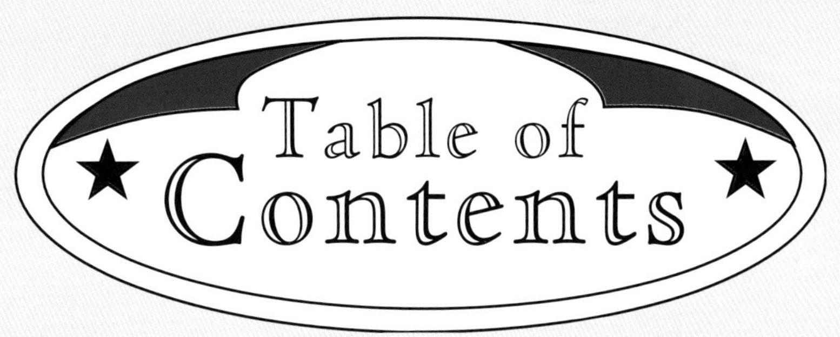

Introduction 6
Arthur M. Schlesinger jr.

The Election of 1828 17
Robert V. Remini

Facts at a Glance 36

First Inaugural Address 41

The Indian Removal Act of 1830 47

Jackson's Volunteer Toast 51

Veto of the Maysville Road Bill 53

Jackson Vetoes the Second Bank 59

To the People of South Carolina 69

Second Inaugural Address 83

Order to Suppress a Labor Strike 89

Andrew Jackson's Farewell Speech 91

Further Reading 106

Index 108

INTRODUCTION

Arthur M. Schlesinger, Jr.

America suffers from a sort of intermittent fever—what one may call a quintan ague. Every fourth year there come terrible shakings, passing into the hot fit of the presidential election; then follows what physicians call "the interval"; then again the fit.

—James Bryce, *The American Commonwealth* (1888)

Running for president is the central rite in the American political order. It was not always so. *Choosing* the chief magistrate had been the point of the quadrennial election from the beginning, but it took a long while for candidates to *run* for the highest office in the land; that is, to solicit, visibly and actively, the support of the voters. These volumes show through text and illustration how those aspiring to the White House have moved on from ascetic self-restraint to shameless self-merchandising. This work thereby illuminates the changing ways the American people have conceived the role of their President. I hope it will also recall to new generations some of the more picturesque and endearing dimensions of American politics.

The primary force behind the revolution in campaign attitudes and techniques was a development unforeseen by the men who framed the Constitution—the rise of the party system. Party competition was not at all their original intent. Quite the contrary: inspired at one or two removes by Lord Bolingbroke's British tract of half a century earlier, *The Idea of a Patriot King*, the Founding Fathers envisaged a Patriot President, standing above party and faction, representing the whole people, offering the nation nonpartisan leadership virtuously dedicated to the common good.

The ideal of the Patriot President was endangered, the Founding Fathers believed, by twin menaces—factionalism and factionalism's ugly offspring, the demagogue. Party competition would only encourage unscrupulous men to appeal to popular passion and prejudice. Alexander Hamilton in the 71st Federalist bemoaned the plight of the people, "beset as they continually are . . . by the snares of the ambitious, the avaricious, the desperate, by the artifices of men who possess their confidence more than they deserve it, and of those who seek to possess rather than to deserve it."

Pervading the Federalist was a theme sounded explicitly both in the first paper and the last: the fear that unleashing popular passions would bring on "the military despotism of a victorious demagogue." If the "mischiefs of faction" were, James Madison admitted in the Tenth Federalist, "sown in the nature of man," the object of politics was to repress this insidious disposition, not to yield to it. "If I could not go to heaven but with a party," said Thomas Jefferson, "I would not go there at all."

So the Father of his Country in his Farewell Address solemnly warned his countrymen against "the baneful effects of the spirit of party." That spirit, Washington conceded, was "inseparable from our nature"; but for popular government it was "truly their worst enemy." The "alternate domination of one faction over another," Washington said, would lead in the end to "formal and permanent despotism." The spirit of a party, "a fire not to be quenched . . . demands a uniform vigilance to prevent its bursting into a flame, lest, instead of warming, it should consume."

Yet even as Washington called on Americans to "discourage and restrain" the spirit of party, parties were beginning to crystallize around him. The eruption of partisanship in defiance of such august counsel argued that party competition might well serve functional necessities in the democratic republic.

After all, honest disagreement over policy and principle called for candid debate. And parties, it appeared, had vital roles to play in the consummation of the Constitution. The distribution of powers among three equal branches inclined the national government toward a chronic condition of stalemate. Parties offered the means of overcoming the constitutional separation of powers by coordinating the executive and legislative branches and furnishing the connective tissue essential to effective government. As national associations, moreover, parties were a force against provincialism and separatism. As instruments of compromise, they encouraged, within the parties as well as between them, the containment and mediation of national quarrels, at least until slavery broke the parties up. Henry D. Thoreau cared little enough for politics, but he saw the point: "Politics is, as it were, the gizzard of society, full of grit and gravel, and the two political parties are its two opposite halves, which grind on each other."

Furthermore, as the illustrations in these volumes so gloriously remind us, party competition was a great source of entertainment and fun—all the more important in those faraway days before the advent of baseball and football, of movies and radio and television. "To take a hand in the regulation of society and to discuss it," Alexis de Tocqueville observed when he visited America in the 1830s, "is his biggest concern and, so to speak, the only pleasure an American knows. . . . Even the women frequently attend public meetings and listen to political harangues as a recreation from their household labors. Debating clubs are, to a certain extent, a substitute for theatrical entertainments."

Condemned by the Founding Fathers, unknown to the Constitution, parties nonetheless imperiously forced themselves into political life. But the party system rose from the bottom up. For half a century, the first half-dozen Presidents continued to hold themselves above party. The disappearance of the Federalist Party after the War of 1812 suspended party competition. James Monroe, with no opponent at all in the election of 1820, presided proudly over the Era of Good Feelings, so called because there were no parties around to excite ill feelings. Monroe's successor, John Quincy Adams, despised electioneering and inveighed against the "fashion of peddling for popularity by

traveling around the country gathering crowds together, hawking for public dinners, and spouting empty speeches." Men of the old republic believed presidential candidates should be men who already deserved the people's confidence rather than those seeking to win it. Character and virtue, not charisma and ambition, should be the grounds for choosing a President.

Adams was the last of the old school. Andrew Jackson, by beating him in the 1828 election, legitimized party politics and opened a new political era. The rationale of the new school was provided by Jackson's counselor and successor, Martin Van Buren, the classic philosopher of the role of party in the American democracy. By the time Van Buren took his own oath of office in 1837, parties were entrenched as the instruments of American self-government. In Van Buren's words, party battles "rouse the sluggish to exertion, give increased energy to the most active intellect, excite a salutary vigilance over our public functionaries, and prevent that apathy which has proved the ruin of Republics."

Apathy may indeed have proved the ruin of republics, but rousing the sluggish to exertion proved, ironically, the ruin of Van Buren. The architect of the party system became the first casualty of the razzle-dazzle campaigning the system quickly generated. The Whigs' Tippecanoe-and-Tyler-too campaign of 1840 transmuted the democratic Van Buren into a gilded aristocrat and assured his defeat at the polls. The "peddling for popularity" John Quincy Adams had deplored now became standard for party campaigners.

But the new methods were still forbidden to the presidential candidates themselves. The feeling lingered from earlier days that stumping the country in search of votes was demagoguery beneath the dignity of the presidency. Van Buren's code permitted—indeed expected—parties to inscribe their creed in platforms and candidates to declare their principles in letters published in newspapers. Occasionally candidates—William Henry Harrison in 1840, Winfield Scott in 1852—made a speech, but party surrogates did most of the hard work.

As late as 1858, Van Buren, advising his son John, one of the great popular orators of the time, on the best way to make it to the White House, emphasized the "rule . . . that the people will never make a man President who is so importunate as to show by his life and conversation that he not only has an eye on, but is in active pursuit of the office. . . . No man who has laid himself out for it, and was unwise enough to let the people into his secret, ever yet obtained it. Clay, Calhoun, Webster, Scott, and a host of lesser lights, should serve as a guide-post to future aspirants."

The continuing constraint on personal campaigning by candidates was reinforced by the desire of party managers to present their nominees as all things to all men. In 1835 Nicholas Biddle, the wealthy Philadelphian who had been Jackson's mortal opponent in the famous Bank War, advised the Whigs not to let General Harrison "say one single word about his principles or his creed. . . . Let him say nothing, promise nothing. Let no committee, no convention, no town meeting ever extract from him a single word about what he thinks now, or what he will do hereafter. Let the use of pen and ink be wholly forbidden as if he were a mad poet in Bedlam."

We cherish the memory of the famous debates in 1858 between Abraham Lincoln and Stephen A. Douglas. But those debates were not part of a presidential election. When the presidency was at stake two years later, Lincoln gave no campaign speeches on the issues darkly dividing the country. He even expressed doubt about party platforms—"the formal written platform system," as he called it. The candidate's character and record, Lincoln thought, should constitute his platform: "On just such platforms all our earlier and better Presidents were elected."

However, Douglas, Lincoln's leading opponent in 1860, foreshadowed the future when he broke the sound barrier and dared venture forth on thinly disguised campaign tours. Yet Douglas established no immediate precedent. Indeed, half a dozen years later Lincoln's successor, Andrew Johnson, discredited presidential stumping by his "swing around the circle" in the midterm

election of 1866. “His performances in a western tour in advocacy of his own election,” commented Benjamin F. Butler, who later led the fight in Congress for Johnson’s impeachment, “. . . disgusted everybody.” The tenth article of impeachment charged Johnson with bringing “the high office of the President of the United States into contempt, ridicule, and disgrace” by delivering “with a loud voice certain intemperate, inflammatory, and scandalous harangues . . . peculiarly indecent and unbecoming in the Chief Magistrate of the United States.”

Though presidential candidates Horatio Seymour in 1868, Rutherford B. Hayes in 1876, and James A. Garfield in 1880 made occasional speeches, only Horace Greeley in 1872, James G. Blaine in 1884, and most spectacularly, William Jennings Bryan in 1896 followed Douglas’s audacious example of stumping the country. Such tactics continued to provoke disapproval. Bryan, said John Hay, who had been Lincoln’s private secretary and was soon to become McKinley’s secretary of state, “is begging for the presidency as a tramp might beg for a pie.”

Respectable opinion still preferred the “front porch” campaign, employed by Garfield, by Benjamin Harrison in 1888, and most notably by McKinley in 1896. Here candidates received and addressed numerous delegations at their own homes—a form, as the historian Gil Troy writes, of “stumping in place.”

While candidates generally continued to stand on their dignity, popular campaigning in presidential elections flourished in these years, attaining new heights of participation (82 percent of eligible voters in 1876 and never once from 1860 to 1900 under 70 percent) and new wonders of pyrotechnics and ballyhoo. Parties mobilized the electorate as never before, and political iconography was never more ingenious and fantastic. “Politics, considered not as the science of government, but as the art of winning elections and securing office,” wrote the keen British observer James Bryce, “has reached in the United States a development surpassing in elaborateness that of England or France as much as the methods of those countries surpass the methods of

Servia or Roumania." Bryce marveled at the "military discipline" of the parties, at "the demonstrations, the parades and receptions, the badges and brass bands and triumphal arches," at the excitement stirred by elections—and at "the disproportion that strikes a European between the merits of the presidential candidate and the blazing enthusiasm which he evokes."

Still the old taboo held back the presidential candidates themselves. Even so irrepressible a campaigner as President Theodore Roosevelt felt obliged to hold his tongue when he ran for reelection in 1904. This unwonted abstinence reminded him, he wrote in considerable frustration, of the July day in 1898 when he was "lying still under shell fire" during the Spanish-American War. "I have continually wished that I could be on the stump myself."

No such constraint inhibited TR, however, when he ran again for the presidency in 1912. Meanwhile, and for the first time, *both* candidates in 1908—Bryan again, and William Howard Taft—actively campaigned for the prize. The duties of the office, on top of the new requirements of campaigning, led Woodrow Wilson to reflect that same year, four years before he himself ran for President, "Men of ordinary physique and discretion cannot be Presidents and live, if the strain be not somehow relieved. We shall be obliged always to be picking our chief magistrates from among wise and prudent athletes,—a small class."

Theodore Roosevelt and Woodrow Wilson combined to legitimate a new conception of presidential candidates as active molders of public opinion in active pursuit of the highest office. Once in the White House, Wilson revived the custom, abandoned by Jefferson, of delivering annual state of the union addresses to Congress in person. In 1916 he became the first incumbent President to stump for his own reelection.

The activist candidate and the bully-pulpit presidency were expressions of the growing democratization of politics. New forms of communication were reconfiguring presidential campaigns. In the nineteenth century the press, far more fiercely partisan then than today, had been the main carrier of political information. In the twentieth century the spread of advertising techniques and the rise of the electronic media—radio, television, computerized public opinion polling—wrought drastic changes in the methodology of politics. In particular the electronic age diminished and now threatens to dissolve the historic role of the party.

The old system had three tiers: the politician at one end; the voter at the other; and the party in between. The party's function was to negotiate between the politician and the voters, interpreting each to the other and providing the link that held the political process together. The electric revolution has substantially abolished the sovereignty of the party. Where once the voter turned to the local party leader to find out whom to support, now he looks at television and makes up his own mind. Where once the politician turned to the local party leader to find out what people are thinking, he now takes a computerized poll.

The electronic era has created a new breed of professional consultants, "handlers," who by the 1980s had taken control of campaigns away from the politicians. The traditional pageantry—rallies, torchlight processions, volunteers, leaflets, billboards, bumper stickers—is now largely a thing of the past. Television replaces the party as the means of mobilizing the voter. And as the party is left to wither on the vine, the presidential candidate becomes more pivotal than ever. We shall see the rise of personalist movements, founded not on historic organizations but on compelling personalities, private fortunes, and popular frustrations. Without the stabilizing influence of parties, American politics would grow angrier, wilder, and more irresponsible.

Things have changed considerably from the austerities of the old republic. Where once voters preferred to call presumably reluctant candidates to the duties of the supreme magistracy and rejected pursuit of the office as evidence of dangerous ambition, now they expect candidates to come to them, explain their views and plead for their support. Where nonpartisan virtue had been the essence, now candidates must prove to voters that they have the requisite "fire in the belly." "'Twud be inth'restin," said Mr. Dooley, ". . . if th' fathers iv th' counthry cud come back an' see what has happened while they've been away. In times past whin ye voted f'r prisident ye didn't vote f'r a man. Ye voted f'r a kind iv a statue that ye'd put up in ye'er own mind on a marble pidistal. Ye nivir heerd iv George Wash'nton goin' around th' counthry distributin' five cint see-gars."

We have reversed the original notion that ambition must be disguised and the office seek the man. Now the man—and soon, one must hope, the woman—seeks the office and does so without guilt or shame or inhibition. This is not necessarily a degradation of democracy. Dropping the disguise is a gain for candor, and personal avowals of convictions and policies may elevate and educate the electorate.

On the other hand, the electronic era has dismally reduced both the intellectual content of campaigns and the attention span of audiences. In the nineteenth century political speeches lasted for a couple of hours and dealt with issues in systematic and exhaustive fashion. Voters drove wagons for miles to hear Webster and Clay, Bryan and Teddy Roosevelt, and felt cheated if the famous orator did not give them their money's worth. Then radio came along and cut political addresses down first to an hour, soon to thirty minutes—still enough time to develop substantive arguments.

But television has shrunk the political talk first to fifteen minutes, now to the sound bite and the thirty-second spot. Advertising agencies today sell candidates with all the cynical contrivance they previously devoted to selling detergents and mouthwash. The result is the debasement of American politics. "The idea that you can merchandise candidates for high office like breakfast cereal," Adlai Stevenson said in 1952, "is the ultimate indignity to the democratic process."

Still Bryce's "intermittent fever" will be upon us every fourth year. We will continue to watch wise if not always prudent athletes in their sprint for the White House, enjoy the quadrennial spectacle and agonize about the outcome.

"The strife of the election," said Lincoln after his reelection in 1864, "is but human-nature practically applied to the facts. What has occurred in this case, must ever recur in similar cases. Human-nature will not change."

Lincoln, as usual, was right. Despite the transformation in political methods there remains a basic continuity in political emotions. "For a long while before the appointed time has come," Tocqueville wrote more than a century and a half ago, "the election becomes the important and, so to speak, the all-engrossing topic of discussion. Factional ardor is redoubled, and all the artificial passions which the imagination can create in a happy and peaceful land are agitated and brought to light. . . .

"As the election draws near, the activity of intrigue and the agitation of the populace increase; the citizens are divided into hostile camps, each of which assumes the name of its favorite candidate; the whole nation glows with feverish excitement; the election is the daily theme of the press, the subject of every private conversation, the end of every thought and every action, the sole interest of the present.

"It is true," Tocqueville added, "that as soon as the choice is determined, this ardor is dispelled, calm returns, and the river, which had nearly broken its banks, sinks to its usual level; but who can refrain from astonishment that such a storm should have arisen?"

The election storm in the end blows fresh and clean. With the tragic exception of 1860, the American people have invariably accepted the result and given the victor their hopes and blessings. For all its flaws and follies, democracy abides.

Let us now turn the pages and watch the gaudy parade of American presidential politics pass by in all its careless glory.

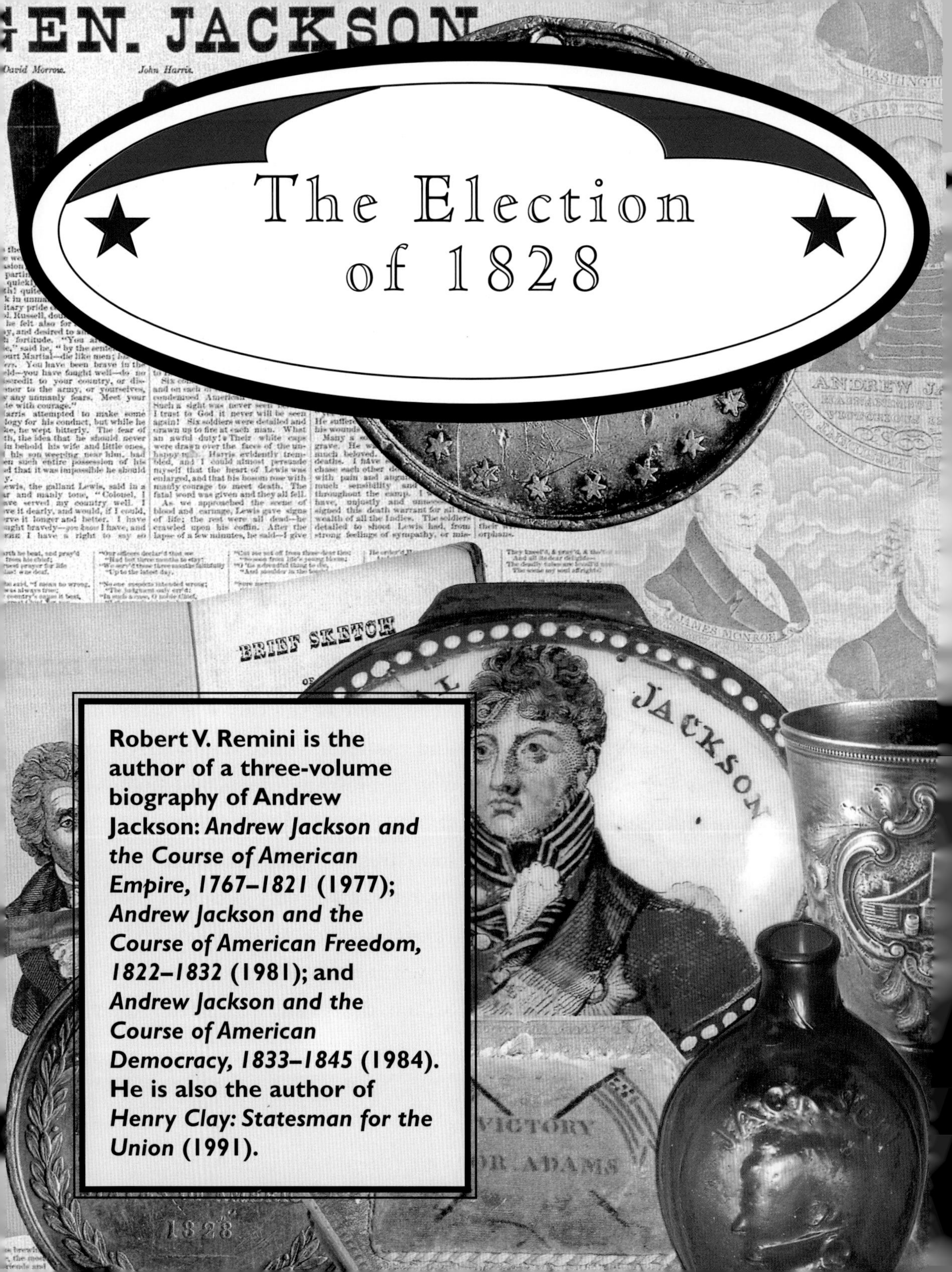

The Election of 1828

Robert V. Remini is the author of a three-volume biography of Andrew Jackson: *Andrew Jackson and the Course of American Empire, 1767–1821* (1977); *Andrew Jackson and the Course of American Freedom, 1822–1832* (1981); and *Andrew Jackson and the Course of American Democracy, 1833–1845* (1984). He is also the author of *Henry Clay: Statesman for the Union* (1991).

During the presidential election of 1828, a new style of political campaigning emerged, one that has since become very typical of American elections. The smear and slander tactics, the hoopla and nonsense to attract voter interest initiated by the newly organized Democratic Party and its opposition, the National Republican Party, constitute only one aspect of the innovations of 1828. The type of presidential candidate—military heroes, for example, rather than experienced and proven statesmen—and the organizational style developed to conduct their campaigns helped form many of the modern methods by which present-day political parties go about nominating and electing the nation's chief executive.

The previous election had been a four-way contest with each candidate running without a party label. All four—John Quincy Adams of Massachusetts, Henry Clay of Kentucky, Andrew Jackson of Tennessee, and William H. Crawford of Georgia—claimed membership in and loyalty to the old Republican Party of Thomas Jefferson and James Madison. None received a majority of electoral votes required by the Constitution and so the election went to the House of Representatives where John Quincy Adams, with the help of Henry Clay, was chosen the sixth president of the United States. Andrew Jackson, who had a plurality of popular and electoral votes in the election and seemed to be the favored choice, charged Adams and Clay with a "corrupt bargain" to defeat the will of the people. "There was *cheating,* and *corruption,*" stormed Jackson, "and *bribery* too." None of these charges was ever proved but the cry of a "corrupt bargain" between the "coalition" of Adams and Clay became the central issue of the 1828 campaign when Adams ran for a second term as candidate of what became known as the National Republican Party. Jackson ran against him as candidate of the Democratic-Republican, or simply the Democratic, party.

Pewter medal. Many of these tokens had holes punched or drilled through the top enabling them to be worn on a chain or ribbon.

Many of the leaders of this revitalized two-party system—Democrats such as Martin Van Buren, John C. Calhoun, Thomas Hart Benton, and National Republicans such as Henry Clay and Daniel Webster—were skillful leaders and politicians. They placed great emphasis on the value of the party system to perpetuate republican principles and maintain stability in government; they espoused party discipline; they organized correspondence committees, local political clubs, and statewide conventions; and they arranged parades, barbecues, tree plantings, street rallies, and all manner of hoopla to control and direct the great masses of voters recently enfranchised by the liberalization of several state constitutions throughout the 1820s, especially after the last election.

Organized support for General Jackson began in the winter of 1826–27 with an agreement between Calhoun and Van Buren to bring together their respective constituencies, namely "the planters of the South and

Brass token from the 1824 election. These tokens or medalets were among the first mass-produced campaign souvenirs.

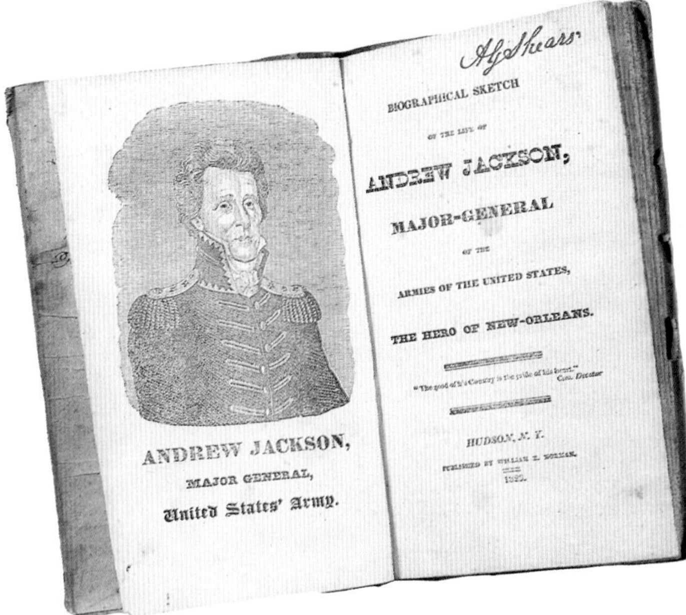

ANDREW JACKSON,
MAJOR GENERAL,
United States' Army.

BIOGRAPHICAL SKETCH
OF THE LIFE OF
ANDREW JACKSON,
MAJOR-GENERAL
OF THE
ARMIES OF THE UNITED STATES,
THE HERO OF NEW-ORLEANS.

HUDSON, N. Y.

This 1828 biography of Andrew Jackson glorifies his military achievements.

plain Republicans of the North," and thereby provide what Van Buren called "the substantial reorganization of the old Republican Party." Following this initial meeting a series of congressional conferences were reportedly held in which "schemes [were] devised, questions debated & the minority was ruled by the majority." They agreed to commence their labors to elect Jackson on July 4, 1827, "in every part of the Union at once." In Nashville, Tennessee, Jackson's hometown, a Central Committee was formed "for the purpose of corresponding with other Jackson committees in the different sections of the country." And so began the elaborate task of structuring a national organization of committees at every political level and in all the states to defeat John Quincy Adams and replace him in the White House with Andrew Jackson.

Attuned to the mood and aspirations of the greatest number of Americans, the Democrats showed uncommon political shrewdness and wisdom by supporting a candidate who was a national hero of unparalleled

Jackson whiskey flask with a portrait of Washington on the reverse. There are twelve different flasks picturing Andrew Jackson.

popularity rather than simply a well-known politician. Andrew Jackson's tremendous victory over the British at New Orleans during the war of 1812 won the admiration, respect, and devotion of the American people as no one had ever done before, not even George Washington. "The *Hurra Boys*," remarked one National Republican, "were for Jackson . . . and all the noisy *Turbulent Boisterous* Politicians are with him and to my regret they constitute a powerful host." The Hurra Boys appropriated Jackson's nickname, "Old Hickory," which gave the party a usable symbol for campaign purposes. Local Democratic organizations were called "Hickory Clubs." Hickory trees were planted during rallies; hats sported hickory leaves; and hickory walking canes, brooms, and buttons with hickory symbols were introduced by the party as a means of designating political preference. The raising of a hickory pole was quite common throughout the campaign of 1828. They appeared "in every village," reported one man, on steeples, on signposts, "as well as upon the corners of many city streets. . . . Many of these poles were standing as late as 1845, rotten momentoes [sic] of the delirium of 1828."

"Planting hickory trees!" snorted one outraged opposition newspaper. "Odds nuts and drumsticks! What have hickory trees to do with republicanism and the great contest?"

In addition to the hickory symbol the Democrats also employed Jackson's likeness on a wide variety of material objects, such as ceramic plates, snuff boxes, pitchers, badges, bandannas, and ladies' hair combs.

Once in a while the "corrupt bargain" might be mentioned on these items but most of them usually referred to the Battle of New Orleans or Jackson's participation as a messenger boy during the American Revolution. They all had the happy effort of linking indelibly in the public mind Old Hickory's name with the nation's glorious past.

Organized barbecues were another means of exciting voter interest. Said one leader, obviously referring to National Republicans: "Those who fear to grease their fingers with a barbecued pig, or twist their mouths away at whisky grog, or start at the fame of a 'military chieftain' [as Jackson was sneeringly referred to by Henry Clay and other National Republicans] or are deafened by the thunder of the canon [sic], may stay away."

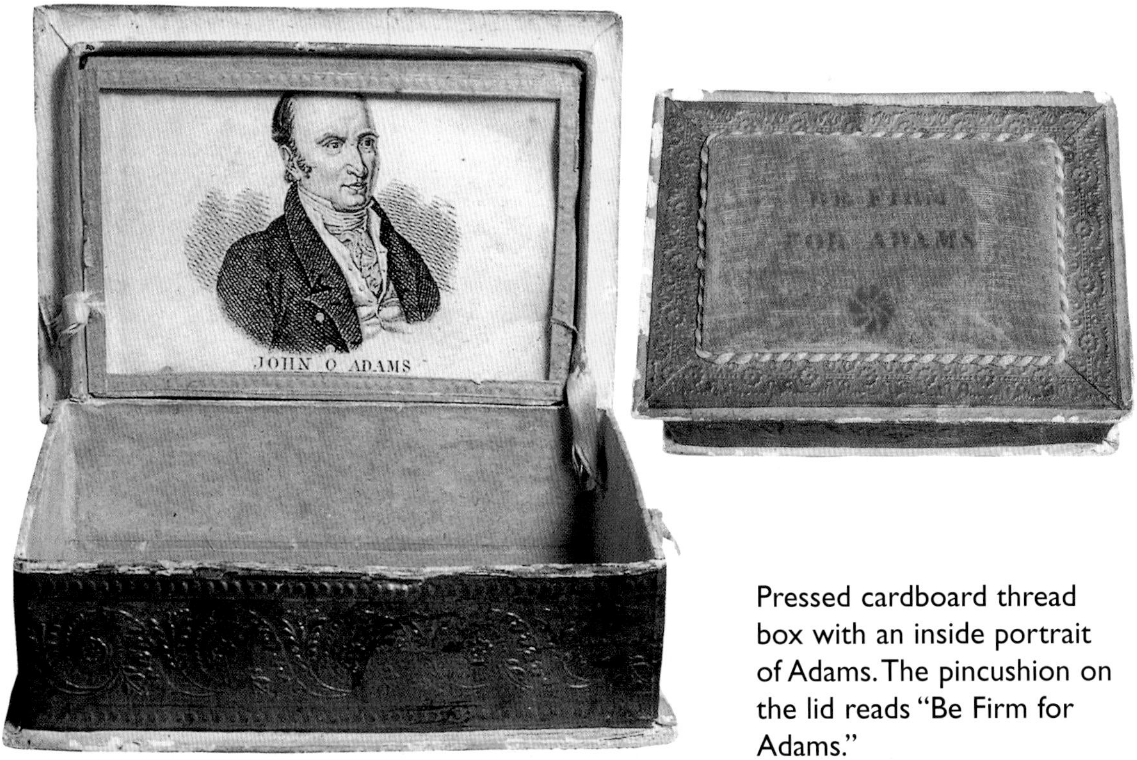

Pressed cardboard thread box with an inside portrait of Adams. The pincushion on the lid reads "Be Firm for Adams."

Reverse painting on glass of General Andrew Jackson. In 1824, Jackson became the first presidential candidate to win a plurality of votes without receiving a majority of the electoral votes.

One such "Grand Barbecue" was held in Baltimore to commemorate the successful defense of the city against British attack during the War of 1812, but it soon became a rally for Jackson. "I am told by a gentleman who is employed to erect the fixtures," Jackson was informed, "that three Bullocks are to be roasted, and each man is to wear a Hickory Leaf in his hat by way of designation." The festivities commenced with the firing of a cannon, followed by a parade of 700 marshals, after which there were speeches, the singing of several songs in praise of Old Hickory, and then the splendid repast of barbecued bullock provided by the Democratic organizers presided over by Roger B. Taney.

On one occasion Jackson himself took part in these demonstrations, although it was considered grossly improper for a candidate to participate actively in his own campaign. "You *must*, I say, you *must* visit us next autumn in person," wrote an Ohio organizer to the general. But Jackson

graciously declined, as he did many other such invitations. However, he did accept the request of the Louisiana Central Committee to attend ceremonies in New Orleans on January 8, 1828, to mark the thirteenth anniversary of his victory over the British in 1815. Presumably it was a national celebration, not a political rally, so Jackson accepted.

But, in fact, it did turn out to be a political rally of extravagant proportions. It was "like a Dream," recorded one man. "The World has never witnessed so glorious, so wonderful a Celebration—never has *Gratitude & Patriotism* so happily united, so beautifully blended—& it will form a bright page in American history." When the Hero of New Orleans arrived by steamboat in the crescent city a huge crowd, numbering in the thousands, had been waiting anxiously for him at the levee beside the Mississippi River. When they finally spotted him aboard his steamboat they started screaming in unison, "Huzza! Huzza! Huzza!" as artillery

ADAMS MEETING.

THE Citizens of Newburyport and Vicinity, friendly to the Election of **JOHN QUINCY ADAMS** to the Presidency, and who prefer him to any other Candidate, are requested to meet at the Town-Hall, ***THIS EVENING***, at half past 6 o'clock, to adopt such measures as may be thought necessary to secure for him a full vote at the approaching election.

☞ *It is expected that there will be a general attendance of the* Citizens *thus disposed, without respect to* party *distinctions.*

ARTHUR GILMAN,
JOHN COFFIN,
BENJ. G. SWEETSER,
GREENE SANBORN,
NATHAN FOLLANSBEE,
ROBERT B. WILLIAMS,
COMMITTEE.

Newburyport, October 30th, 1824.

An 1824 meeting announcement for supporters of John Quincy Adams.

As popular voting increased, new artifacts were introduced to promote candidates, images, and slogans. Pewter medalets remained popular until the 1876 election.

"thundered from the land and the water." There followed welcoming speeches, a parade through the French quarter and a splendid dinner in the evening. For four days the celebration continued, and at every opportunity the glorious battle of January 8 was recounted in French and English, all of which was duly reported in the Democratic newspapers throughout the country. The American people were thus reminded that in their hour of greatest peril General Jackson, "the soldier boy of the Revolution," stepped forward and "saved" the nation from possible destruction.

The delight to which the public responded to this new brand of electioneering encouraged party leaders to devise a wide range of entertainments, such as songs, marches, funny stories, poems, puns, and

cartoons. For the Democrats the songs and marches naturally focused on the Battle of New Orleans. Probably the most popular song was "The Hunters of Kentucky" with verses by Samuel Woodworth and adapted by Noah M. Ludlow to a melody from the comic opera *Love Laughs at Locksmiths*. The song invariably had the effect of rousing an audience to near-hysterical shouts of praise for Old Hickory and the men who fought with him. Two lively stanzas of this song, which included mention of the defeated British commander, Sir Michael Pakenham, went as follows:

> You've heard, I s'pose, of New Orleans,
>   'Tis famed for youth and beauty,
> They've girls of every hue, it seems,
>   From snowy white to sooty,
> Now Pakenham had made his brags,
>   If he that day was lucky,
> He'd have those girls and cotton bags
>   In spite of Old Kentucky. . . .
>
> But Jackson he was wide awake,
>   And was not scared at trifles,
> For well he knew Kentucky's boys,
>   With their death-dealing rifles,
> He led them down to cypress swamp,
>   The ground was low and mucky,
> There stood John Bull in martial pomp,
>   And here stood Old Kentucky.
>
> Oh! Kentucky, the hunters of Kentucky!
> Oh! Kentucky, the hunters of Kentucky!

Other songs and marches included "Hickory Wood," "The Battle of New Orleans," and the "General Jackson March" and these were sung and marched to at street rallies, local meetings and conventions, and in taverns and hotels around the country.

The jokes and puns were uniformly terrible but they apparently served a purpose. Some samples include the following:

> "Hurray for *Jackson*," cried one man.
> "Hurrah for the Devil," responded a National Republican.
> "Very well," replied the Democrat. "You stick to your candidate, and I'll stick to mine."
>
> *Question:* "Why is Adams on ticklish grounds?"
> *Answer:* "Because he stands on slippery Clay."

One "funny" story that made the newspaper rounds accused the National Republicans of acting like the Frenchman who boasted that King Louis had spoken to him.

> "What did the King say to you?" asked an envious friend.
> "He told me to get out of his way," replied the delighted Frenchman.

In their campaign propaganda Democrats regularly depicted Adams as the candidate of the aristocracy who strolled through the White House like a king and recklessly spent the people's taxes on the trappings of royalty. "We disapprove," cried the Democratic press, "the kingly pomp and splendour that is displayed by the present incumbent." As proof evidence was advanced to show that $25,000 of public funds had been used to equip the White House with gambling furniture, including billiard table, cues, balls, backgammon board, dice, and a set of expensive chessmen made of ivory. Clearly, such mindless nonsense about cues and balls and chessmen was meant to demonstrate that the Democratic Party, in the name of the American people, was engaged in a struggle against privilege and wealth.

"The Aristocracy and the Democracy of the country are arrayed against each other," declared one Jacksonian.

Secretary of State Henry Clay, noted for his American System to encourage the development of domestic manufactures and industry, was also denounced for his extravagant tastes. He reputedly used English writing paper in his department! "O fie, Mr. Clay—*English* paper, *English* wax, *English* pen-knives, is this your *American System*?"

Ethnic and religious bigotry also raised an ugly head in this election. In cities where it might generate votes, Democratic newspapers reminded their readers that Jackson was "the son of honest Irish parents. . . . That natural interest which all true hearted Irishmen feel in the fame of one who has so much genuine Irish blood in his veins, had drawn down upon the heads of that devoted people, the denunciations of the partisans of

The obverse and reverse of an 1828 medal: "Advocate of the American System." Indeed a strange slogan for Andrew Jackson. Nevertheless, in the 1828 campaign, he was acclaimed as a frontier hero, a symbol of the common man, and a supporter of the "American System."

American Statesman Extra.

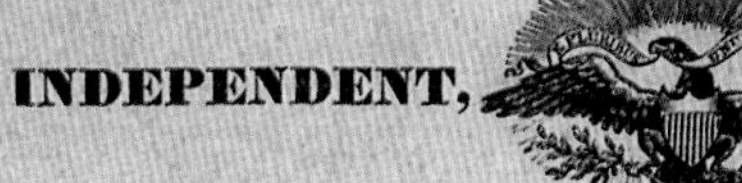

INDEPENDENT, UNPLEDGED,

NATIONAL REPUBLICAN

Electoral Ticket.

Rev. THOMAS BALDWIN, D. D.
Hon. WILLIAM BAYLIES. } *Electors at large.*

Hon. WM. WALKER, *Berkshire District.*
Gen. SAMUEL PORTER, *Franklin.*
Dr. TIMOTHY HORTON, *Hampden.*
Hon. SOLOMON STRONG, *Worcester North.*
Dr. DANIEL THURBER, *Worcester South.*
Hon. EDMUND FOSTER, *Middlesex.*
DAVID HOW, Esq. *Essex North.*
WILLIAM SUTTON, Esq. *Essex South.*
Hon. SAMUEL HUBBARD, *Suffolk.*
Hon. BENJAMIN REYNOLDS, *Norfolk.*
Hon. JOHN M. WILLIAMS, *Bristol.*
BENJAMIN HOBART, Esq. *Plymouth.*
NYMPHAS MARSTON, Esq. *Barnstable.*

To the Independent Electors of Massachusetts.

THE undersigned, chosen as a Central Committee for the State, at a meeting of the citizens of Boston, and in pursuance of the request of the Convention in Berkshire, for the purpose of communicating with the people in the various districts of the Commonwealth, relative to a nomination of unpledged candidates as electors of President and Vice President, were instructed by their constituents to publish, in their behalf, an address to you. The time approaches, fellow citizens, when an election of the highest importance under the government of the United States must take place; and the part you are to act is not only of consequence to you, but to the reputation of the state, and to the interests of the community. A majority of your representatives, at the last session of the Legislature, passed a law, that the electors of President in Massachusetts should be chosen by a general ticket; and a portion of those representatives soon after met in *Caucus*, and designated the candidates to be voted for for that high and responsible trust. We did suppose the past history of this Commonwealth would have saved us from so daring an encroachment upon our rights. Your sentiments could not have been mistaken by them, for in 1804, at a period when the excited passions of men urged them to the extreme bounds of propriety and good faith, you solemnly proclaimed the measure to be destitute of principle, and an usurpation on your rights. The opposition you then made to this odious law is one of the noblest acts recorded on your political annals, as it proves that neither the ardour of excited passions, nor the discipline of party, could seduce you from an adherance to principle, or a regard for justice. The act was adopted by the party which the majority of the people then supported, but the stern integrity of the people themselves rejected the measure of their representatives, and sacrificed the ascendancy of party to the preservation of justice. There was something in the conduct of many federalists on that occasion worthy at once of our respect and imitation. They were told, as the noble Aristides told the people of Athens, that the measure would be beneficial to them, but would not be just; and like the illustrious Athenians, they replied, "we seek justice before our interests." The protest of a republican minority was nobly sustained by many federalists as well as by the republican party: and the attempt to build up a party ascendancy, by trampling on the rights of a minority, was put down, in part, by those for whose benefit it was intended.

After so deliberate an expression of the will of the people, it is not without surprise, fellow citizens, that we have recently beheld another Legislature emboldened to the repetition of a similar attempt; and if any thing could add to the astonishment which is excited when the wishes of the people are disregarded their representatives, it would be that the party which now renews the attempt, is that which entered its protest against it in 1804. In addition to the protest of the minority of the Senate, *one hundred and one members* of the House of Representatives, made a solemn remonstrance against the general electoral law, with a request that it might be permanently entered on the records of the House; and among others the following were the reasons which they assigned.

1. "It defeats the *first principle* of the *elective franchise.*"
2. "It is *repugnant to the habits and usages* of the people of this Commonwealth."
3. "It is calculated to open the door to *intrigue, and imposition on the people.*"
4. "It is fallacious on the *face* of it, appearing to give an elector to each district, while it may secure one in direct opposition to the majority of its voters."
5. "*It will deprive one party of their due weight, in the appointment of the first magistrate of the union.*"

Such, fellow citizens, were the sentiments of the republican members of the Legislature in 1804—will it not challenge human credulity to believe, that it is the *republican Legislature* of 1824, by whom a measure which they thus characterised when a minority, is now adopted and defended? Is it they "*who have consented to defeat the first principle of the elective franchise,*" "*to adopt a course repugnant to the habits and usages of the people,*" "*to open the door to intrigue and imposition,*" and "*to deprive the party,*" now in the minority, "*of their due weight in the appointment of the first magistrate of the union*" Is it the *republican party* who practice in power the principles they condemned when out of it; who will oppress the minority who, when they themselves were oppressed, magnanimously interfered in their protection, and sacrificed their own interests in defence of republican rights. Will republican citizens manifest less regard for principle now than federal citizens did in 1804, and show that while their representatives can follow an example they have condemned, the people will not imitate a virtue they admired.

But great as is the outrage of the general ticket law on the usages and feelings of the people of this state, it sinks into insignificance compared with the high-handed measures which followed it. Not content with taking from the people in the districts their ancient right of choosing their own electors, the usurpation was followed up by an act for which the party efforts of this state afford no precedent. A part of the republican members of the Legislature met in *caucus*, and dictated the candidates for whom the people should vote. But not satisfied with taking from districts the right of election, they endeavoured to defeat even the humble privilege *of nominating their candidates;* and, as if it were even too great a concession to the people, that they should be oppressed by their own representatives, a *junto of five* men was created, with power to *change the candidates* if they thought proper, whom the people should be *at liberty to support.* We can follow this train of usurpation, fellow citizens, no farther, without feelings to which we find it difficult for language to give expression. The occasion has shown with what facility men can pass from injury to insult, and add a mockery of the constitution to an outrage on the people. Four of the five members of the junto thus set up by the Legislagre, to guide the people in the choice of *electors*, were men prohibited by the national constitution from choosing a President. The second article, first section of the constitution of the United States, provides, that "no senator, representative, or *person holding an office of trust or profit* under the United States, shall be appointed an elector;" and yet two of the five composing the junto, were representatives in Congress, to wit, Messrs. Crowninshield and Fuller; and two others held offices of "trust and profit" under the United States, Mr. Dearborn, the Collector of Boston, and Mr. Hill, the Postmaster.

If the principles proclaimed by the republican party in 1804, and sanctioned by the people, were right, it was wrong to deprive the districts of the right of choosing their electors, and oppression and injustice to take from the minority in the state "its due weight in the appointment of the first magistrate of the union." No power remained with the people to repeal the law, but there was one right remaining of which no usurpation could deprive them. It was still competent to the people to give or withhold their sanction to the injustice, and to nominate the candidates for whom they would vote. Attempts have indeed been made to awe them into submission, but force and violence have not yet destroyed the last vestige of the elective franchise which is protected by our constitution and laws. To nominate such electors in each district as would express the sentiments of the people, of whatever party they might be, was the only alternative which the law had left open, and we are happy to have it in our power to announce to you that this right has been exercised. The ticket thus made up is composed as the republican protest in 1804, contended it should be, of both political parties, allowing both to the majority and the minority, "their due weight in the appointment of the chief magistrate of the union." The men thus offered for your support are entitled to your confidence, and have generally heretofore received it, for the most important trusts in your power to confer; and the principle which has governed the people in the selection of them, has been, it is believed, invariably, a regard to the political sentiments of the majority in the district for which they were nominated.

We have been compelled to recommend for your support a candidate for the district of Barnstable, without having for the recommendation the previous sanction of the electors of that district, at some public meeting: but the time for the election is so near that much solicitude has been manifested from all parts of the commonwealth, for the immediate publication of the ticket, and the undersigned have not felt at liberty to delay it any longer. In recommending the gentleman for that district, however, we have been guided by such information from the voters in that quarter, as to leave us no reason to doubt that it will meet their cordial approbation and support.

In concluding the remarks which we have felt bound to submit to you, we regret the necessity of adverting to a subject which cannot have failed to excite in your minds, the same sentiments of regret and surprise which it has occasioned to this committee. To say that the unwillingness manifested, at so late a moment after their nomination, by Governors Eustis and Brooks, to stand as candidates, was *unexpected* and extraordinary, is but to express, we believe, the sentiments of all fair and intelligent men. It imposed on this committee, from the impracticability of holding, in each district of the state, an additional meeting of the people, the responsible duty of recommending others in their place. In the discharge of this duty we have communicated with the committees chosen by the people for their several districts, and we feel confident in the assertion, that the names which have been substituted, will, to say the least, be equally acceptable to the people and as auspicious to our success.

The ticket thus offered to you, we hazard nothing in saying, is entitled to as strong a support as any which has been submitted to the people of this commonwealth; and if information from all quarters of the state, and from the most respectable sources, is entitled to credit, we feel authorized to anticipate for it, with due exertion, a decided success.

LEONARD M. PARKER,
EBENEZER SEAVER,
HENRY ORNE,
DAVID HENSHAW,
WILLIAM INGALLS,
SAMUEL BILLINGS,
BARNEY SMITH, } *Central Committee of the State.*

An 1829 political broadside published by a Massachusetts newspaper.

Messrs. Adams & Clay" "Mr. Adams," on the other hand, hated the Irish and "denounced the Roman Catholics as bigots, worshippers of images, and declared that they did not read their bibles." Worse, he was secretly working to "unite CHURCH AND STATE after the manner of the English monarch."

Newspapers played a vital role in propagating and advertising much of the foolishness and hoopla. Early in the campaign Democratic congressmen decided to establish "a chain of newspaper posts, from the New England States to Louisiana, and branching off through Lexington to the Western States." They recognized that a hard-hitting, vigorous press was essential for party success. "We have at considerable expense," wrote one Democrat, "established another newspaper in the northern part of New Hampshire. We have organized our fences in every quarter and have begun & shall continue without ceasing to pour into every doubtful region all kinds of useful information." The best of these Democratic journals included the Washington D.C. *United States Telegraph*, the Richmond *Enquirer,* the Albany *Argus*, the Kentucky *Argus of Western America*, the Boston *Statesman,* the New York *Courier, Inquirer,* and *Evening Post*, and the Charleston *Mercury.* It was estimated that six hundred newspapers operated in this election, fifty of them dailies, a hundred and fifty semi-weeklies, and four hundred weeklies.

Some newspapers stooped to gutter tactics and made libelous charges of explicit sexual misconduct by one or the other candidate. For example, John Quincy Adams was accused

Hand-painted French porcelain bowl with a portrait of John Quincy Adams.

of pimping for the czar of Russia! A brief campaign biography of Jackson published by Isaac Hill, the Democratic organizer of New Hampshire, stated that Adams, when minister to Russia, procured an American girl for the czar. Actually, the girl in question was Martha Godfrey, Mrs. Adams's maid and nurse to young Charles Francis Adams. She wrote letters back home repeating the gossip of the Russian court and including mention of the czar's love affairs. One letter was intercepted and shown to the czar who expressed a wish to see the girl. As it developed, when Charles Francis Adams was presented to the czarina's sister he was accompanied by his nurse. Then, during the presentation, the czar suddenly appeared and spent several minutes talking with the child and the gossipy Martha. John Quincy Adams recorded in his diary that Martha's letter had afforded the czar "some amusement. . . . It was from this trivial incident that this base imputation has been trumped up," he added.

Trumped up or not, the Democrats made excellent political use of it. Adams was mocked as a "pimp" whose fabulous success as a diplomat had at last been explained. "The Pimp of the Coalition" was one of the titles conferred on him by Democrats. Adams was also accused of premarital sex with his wife.

The organization of the National Republican Campaign fell mainly to Clay, Webster, and other leaders in Congress and the states. But their organizing efforts paled alongside those of the Democrats. A meeting of the friends of the Adams administration for the purpose of forming a new party convened in Boston. They were urged to forget the "old political landmarks." Theirs would be a new party but one rooted in the broad tenets of republicanism. Personal factions must end. No longer should the Republican Party be divided among four or more candidates, as had happened in 1824, each claiming to represent the identical party. Said Clay: "It appears to me to be important that we should, on all occasions, inculcate the incontestable truth that *now* there are but two parties in the Union."

French textile, circa 1829. Roller-print bearing likenesses of all the presidents. The frigate *Constitution*, made famous during the War of 1812, appears at the right.

Like the Democrats, National Republican leaders emphasized the importance of a vigorous and hard-hitting press, and by and large Adams was well served. In Washington the *National Intelligencer* and the *National Journal* provided excellent support. Elsewhere in the country

Pewter goblet with the inscription "Jackson's birthplace," which was Waxhaw, South Carolina (March 15, 1767). The log cabin identified Jackson with the common man.

they were echoed by the New York *American*, the Cincinnati *Gazette*, the Virginia *Constitutional Whig*, *Niles Weekly Register* of Baltimore, the Massachusetts *Journal*, the Kentucky *Reporter*, the Illinois *Gazette*, and the Missouri *Republican*, among others.

Several of these sheets turned out powerful editorials, and a few stooped to a new low level of mudslinging, one rarely equaled in American history. The unusual, not to say strange, circumstances of Jackson's marriage to Rachel Donelson Robards received extended notice. The worst paper was the Cincinnati *Gazette*, edited by Charles Hammond with financial support from the National Republican Party through the good offices of Henry Clay. On March 23, 1827, Hammond let fly his first fistful of filth. "In the summer of 1790," he wrote, "Gen. Jackson prevailed upon the wife of Lewis Roberts [Robards] of Mercer county, Kentucky, to desert her husband, and live with himself, in the character of a wife." Under normal circumstances such sexual impropriety would have annihilated Jackson's candidacy. But the Nashville Central Committee responded with documentary evidence that branded the story a complete distortion and fabrication. Jackson and Rachel, the Central Committee contended in a published report, believed that Robards had obtained a

divorce and so they married in Natchez, only to learn later that no divorce had been granted. After the divorce was finally granted in 1793 Jackson and Rachel remarried. Naturally, nothing was said about the Kentucky court that found Rachel guilty of desertion and adultery with another man. Hammond responded to the argument of the Central Committee by asking: "Ought a convicted adulteress and her paramour husband to be placed in the highest offices of this free and christian land?"

The charge devastated both Jackson and Rachel. Shortly after the election Rachel died of a heart attack, brought on, claimed her husband and friends, by lies and slander generated during the campaign.

And it got even worse. In one of the most vicious and unconscionable editorials ever to appear in an American newspaper, Hammond intensified his assault against the Old Hero:

> General Jackson's mother was a COMMON PROSTITUTE, brought to this country by the British soldiers! She afterwards married a MULATTO MAN, with whom she had several children, of which number GENERAL JACKSON IS ONE!!!

Jackson's reputation as a duelist and gunfighter and an all-around ruffian was also given considerable notice in the opposition press. Hammond provided a list of fourteen "juvenile indiscretions" attributed to

United States large copper cent counter-stamped with Adams's name. During the nineteenth century, merchants and politicians used coins and currency for free advertising. This practice was later outlawed.

Probably a trinket or sewing box with a hand-colored lithographed portrait under glass. This unusual item measures but 3-1/2″ by 5″ and is 2″ high.

Jackson between the ages of twenty-three and sixty, involving public brawls, gunfights, duels, stabbing and other acts of mayhem which supposedly documented the general's "*intemperate life and character*." Surely such a man, argued Hammond, was singularly "unfit for the highest civil appointment within the gift of my country."

Hammond's journalistic assaults on Jackson's character were aided by John Binns, editor of the Philadelphia *Democratic Press*, who conceived the so-called "Coffin Hand Bill." This leaflet, entitled "Some Account of Some of the Bloody Deeds of GENERAL JACKSON," described how six militiamen were put to death during the Creek War because they tried to return home at the conclusion of their enlistment. The handbill was bordered in black with six black coffins drawn under the names of six militiamen. In one corner of the handbill Jackson is seen running his sword cane through the back of a man in the act of picking up a stone to defend himself. A grand jury acquitted the general of wrongdoing in this incident when he

pleaded self-defense. “Gentle reader,” said the handbill, “it is for you to say, whether this man, who carries a sword cane, and is willing to run it through the body of any one who may presume to stand in his way, it is a fit person to be our President.”

Other accusations included gambling, cockfighting, drinking, swearing, slave trading, and participating in the Burr Conspiracy. Jackson did in fact build boats for Aaron Burr but swore he never believed or knew that there was a conspiracy to dismember the Union.

And his executions of two British citizens, Robert Ambrister and Alexander Arbuthnot, during the First Seminole War when he seized Florida from the Spanish, was denounced as a lawless act that nearly triggered a war with England.

Jackson won the election of 1828 despite these distorted and frequently manufactured stories of impropriety. He won because the American people loved and trusted him and because the Democratic Party proved to be better organized and run by superior politicians. His inauguration on March 4, 1829, resulted in a popular explosion of joy and happiness that almost wrecked the White House. And although the election inaugurated party management of a mass electorate and produced some of the grossest and most disgusting campaigning in American history, it also marked the beginning of practices whose aim and purpose was to directly involve the American people in the election of their chief executive.

Battersea enamel pillbox. The portrait is not Jackson but of the Marquis de Lafayette. Dating from the War of 1812, this is not a campaign item.

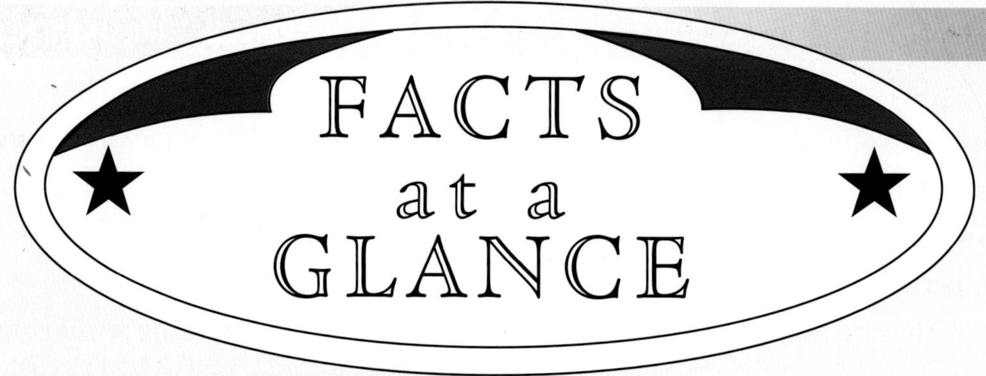

ANDREW JACKSON

- **Born:** March 15, 1767, in Waxhaw, South Carolina
- **Parents:** Andrew and Elizabeth Hutchinson Jackson
- **Education:** no formal education
- **Occupation:** Lawyer, soldier
- **Married:** Rachel Donelson Robards (1767–1828) in August 1791 and in a second ceremony on January 17, 1794
- **Children:** Andrew Jackson Jr. (adopted)
- **Died:** June 8, 1845, at the Hermitage in Nashville, Tennessee

Served as the SEVENTH PRESIDENT OF THE UNITED STATES,

- March 4, 1829, to March 3, 1837

VICE PRESIDENT

- John C. Calhoun, 1829–32
- Martin Van Buren, 1833–37

CABINET

Secretary of State

- Martin Van Buren (1829–31)
- Edward Livingston (1831–33)
- Louis McLane (1833–34)
- John Forsyth (1834–37)

Secretary of the Treasury

- Samuel D. Ingham (1829–31)
- Louis McLane (1831–33)
- William J. Duane (1833)
- Roger B. Taney (1833–34)
- Levi Woodbury (1834–37)

Secretary of War

- John H. Eaton (1829–31)
- Lewis Cass (1831–36)

Attorney General

- John M. Berrien (1829–31)
- Roger B. Taney (1831–33)
- Benjamin F. Butler (1833–37)

Postmaster General

- William T. Barry (1829–35)
- Amos Kendall (1835–37)

Secretary of the Navy

- John Branch (1829–31)
- Levi Woodbury (1831–34)
- Mahlon Dickerson (1834–37)

POLITICAL POSITIONS

- Member of U.S. House of Representatives, 1796–97
- United States Senator, 1797–98
- Justice on Tennessee Supreme Court, 1798–1804
- Governor of the Florida Territory, 1821
- United States Senator, 1823–25
- President of the United States, March 4, 1829, to March 3, 1837

NOTABLE EVENTS DURING JACKSON'S ADMINISTRATION

1829 Jackson gives government jobs to about 2,000 supporters, and sets up a "kitchen cabinet" of informal advisers.

1830 The Indian Removal Act is passed.

1832 Jackson reelected easily, garnering 219 electoral votes and 55 percent of the popular vote in a four-way contest; vetoes the rechartering of the Second Bank of the United States, leading to the creation of the Whig Party; South Carolina attempts to nullify federal tariff laws; Jackson issues his proclamation to the people of South Carolina on December 18.

1834 Federal troops are sent to intervene in a labor strike on the Chesapeake and Ohio Canal, Maryland.

1835 Thanks to a boom in sales of federal lands, the United States pays off its national debt, becoming debt-free for the first time in its history. This lasts only a short time, however.

1836 After the fall of the Alamo in March, the Republic of Texas wins its freedom from Mexico after the battle of San Jacinto; to counter growing land speculation, the Specie Circular, issued July 11, says gold and silver are the only currency acceptable for the purchase of federal lands.

1837 Jackson delivers his farewell address and retires to his home in Tennessee.

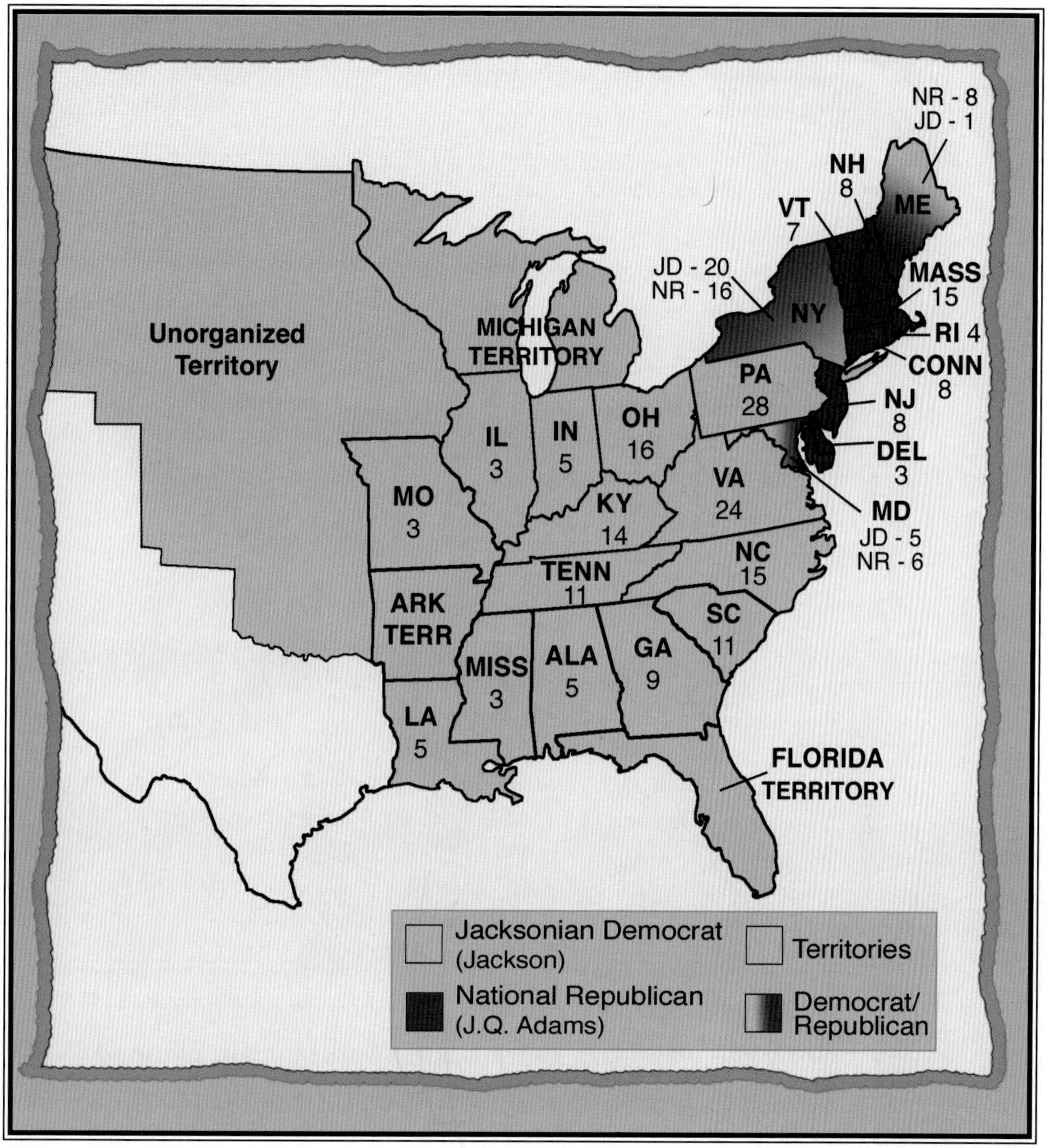

Andrew Jackson easily won the election of 1828 over incumbent John Quincy Adams, collecting 178 electoral votes and 56 percent of the popular vote. Adams, who had defeated Jackson in the much closer 1824 election, received 83 electoral votes in the 1828 election.

First Inaugural Address

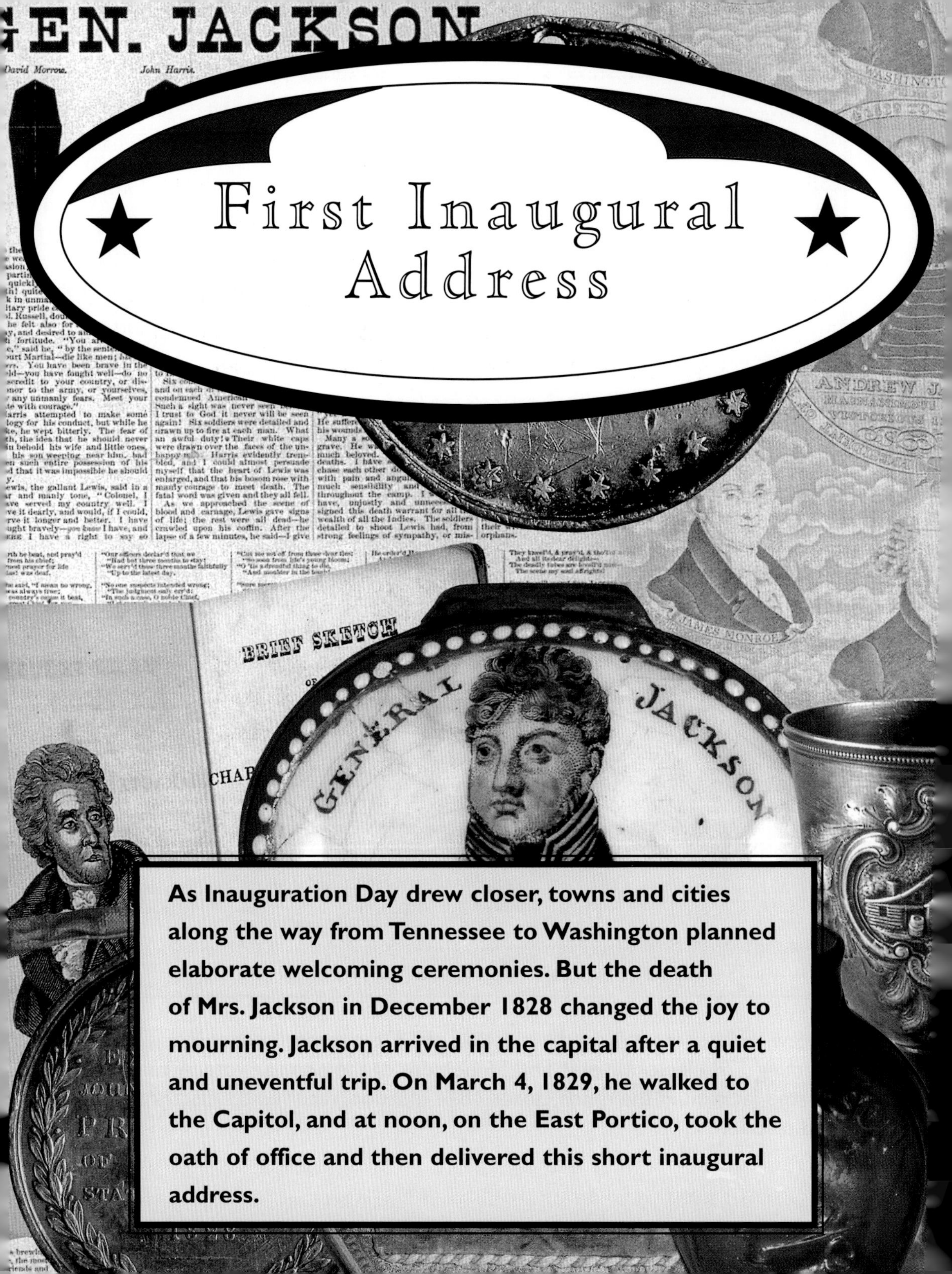

As Inauguration Day drew closer, towns and cities along the way from Tennessee to Washington planned elaborate welcoming ceremonies. But the death of Mrs. Jackson in December 1828 changed the joy to mourning. Jackson arrived in the capital after a quiet and uneventful trip. On March 4, 1829, he walked to the Capitol, and at noon, on the East Portico, took the oath of office and then delivered this short inaugural address.

About to undertake the arduous duties that I have been appointed to perform by the choice of a free people, I avail myself of this customary and solemn occasion to express the gratitude which their confidence inspires and to acknowledge the accountability which my situation enjoins. While the magnitude of their interests convinces me that no thanks can be adequate to the honor they have conferred, it admonishes me that the best return I can make is the zealous dedication of my humble abilities to their service and their good.

As the instrument of the Federal Constitution it will devolve on me for a stated period to execute the laws of the United States, to superintend their foreign and their confederate relations, to manage their revenue, to command their forces, and, by communications to the Legislature, to watch over and to promote their interests generally. And the principles of action by which I shall endeavor to accomplish this circle of duties it is now proper for me briefly to explain.

In administering the laws of Congress I shall keep steadily in view the limitations as well as the extent of the Executive power trusting thereby to discharge the functions of my office without transcending its authority. With foreign nations it will be my study to preserve peace and to cultivate friendship on fair and honorable terms, and in the adjustment of any differences that may exist or arise to exhibit the forbearance becoming a powerful nation rather than the sensibility belonging to a gallant people.

In such measures as I may be called on to pursue in regard to the rights of the separate States I hope to be animated by a proper respect for those sovereign members of our Union, taking care not to confound the powers they have reserved to themselves with those they have granted to the Confederacy.

The management of the public revenue—that searching operation in all governments—is among the most delicate and important trusts in ours, and it will, of course, demand no inconsiderable share of my official solicitude. Under every aspect in which it can be considered it would appear that advantage must result from the observance of a strict and faithful economy. This I shall aim at the more anxiously both because it will facilitate the extinguishment of the national debt, the unnecessary duration of which is incompatible with real independence, and because it will counteract that tendency to public and private profligacy which a profuse expenditure of money by the Government is but too apt to engender. Powerful auxiliaries to the attainment of this desirable end are to be found in the regulations provided by the wisdom of Congress for the specific appropriation of public money and the prompt accountability of public officers.

With regard to a proper selection of the subjects of impost with a view to revenue, it would seem to me that the spirit of equity, caution and compromise in which the Constitution was formed requires that the great interests of agriculture, commerce, and manufactures should be equally favored, and that perhaps the only exception to this rule should consist in the peculiar encouragement of any products of either of them that may be found essential to our national independence.

Internal improvement and the diffusion of knowledge, so far as they can be promoted by the constitutional acts of the Federal Government, are of high importance.

Considering standing armies as dangerous to free governments in time of peace, I shall not seek to enlarge our present establishment, nor disregard that salutary lesson of political experience which teaches that the military should be held subordinate to the civil power. The gradual increase of our Navy, whose flag has displayed in distant climes our skill in navigation and our fame in arms; the preservation of our forts, arsenals, and dockyards, and the introduction of progressive improvements in the discipline and science of both branches of our military service are so plainly prescribed by prudence that I should be excused for omitting their mention sooner than for enlarging

Hexagonal Adams thread box.

John Quincy Adams looked forward to retiring. He had many hobbies to occupy his time, including swimming, playing the flute, and organizing his large library. But only one year after he returned to Massachusetts, local political leaders asked if he would find the office of Congressman too degrading after serving as president. Adams replied, "No person could be degraded by serving the people as a Representative to Congress." He easily won election. In December 1830, Adams returned to Washington, this time as a representative from the 8th district of Massachusetts. He remains the only president to date to serve in the House of Representatives after leaving the White House.

on their importance. But the bulwark of our defense is the national militia, which in the present state of our intelligence and population must render us invincible. As long as our Government is administered for the good of the people, and is regulated by their will; as long as it secures to us the rights of person and of property, liberty of conscience and of the press, it will be worth defending; and so long as it is worth defending a patriotic militia will cover it with an impenetrable aegis. Partial injuries and occasional mortifications we may be subjected to, but a million of armed freemen, possessed of the means of war, can never be conquered by a foreign foe. To any just system, therefore, calculated to strengthen this natural safeguard of the country I shall cheerfully lend all the aid in my power.

It will be my sincere and constant desire to observe toward the Indian tribes within our limits a just and liberal policy, and to give that humane and considerate attention to their rights and their wants which is consistent with the habits of our Government and the feelings of our people.

Rare John Quincy Adams 1825 inaugural medal struck in both silver and pewter. During Adams's 17 years in Congress, he behaved in the same independent way as he had when president. He did not work consistently with any party and he did not make deals with other representatives. He spoke for and stood for only what he thought was right. To a Boston friend he wrote in 1836, "I stand in the House of Representatives, as I stood in the last Congress—alone."

The recent demonstration of public sentiment inscribes on the list of Executive duties, in characters too legible to be overlooked, the task of reform, which will require particularly the correction of those abuses that have brought the patronage of the Federal Government into conflict with the freedom of elections, and the counteraction of those causes which have disturbed the rightful course of appointment and have placed or continued power in unfaithful or incompetent hands.

In the performance of a task thus generally delineated I shall endeavor to select men whose diligence and talents will insure in their respective stations able and faithful cooperation, depending for the advancement of the public service more on the integrity and zeal of the public officers than on their numbers.

A diffidence, perhaps too just, in my own qualifications will teach me to look with reverence to the examples of public virtue left by my illustrious predecessors, and with veneration to the lights that flow from the mind that founded and the mind that reformed our system. The same diffidence induces me to hope for instruction and aid from the coordinate branches of the Government, and for the indulgence and support of my fellow-citizens generally. And a firm reliance on the goodness of that Power whose providence mercifully protected our national infancy, and has since upheld our liberties in various vicissitudes, encourages me to offer up my ardent supplications that He will continue to make our beloved country the object of His divine care and gracious benediction.

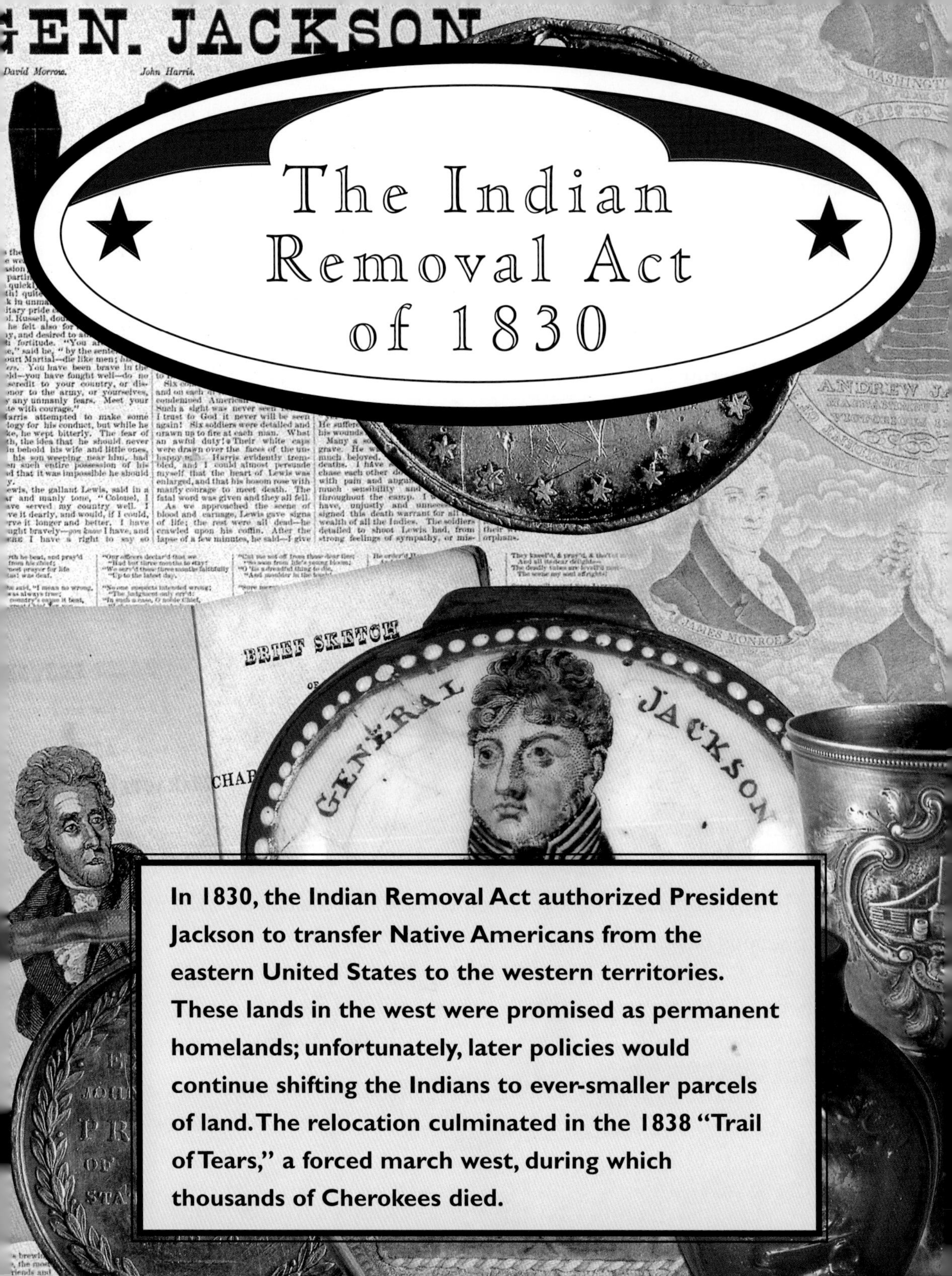

The Indian Removal Act of 1830

In 1830, the Indian Removal Act authorized President Jackson to transfer Native Americans from the eastern United States to the western territories. These lands in the west were promised as permanent homelands; unfortunately, later policies would continue shifting the Indians to ever-smaller parcels of land. The relocation culminated in the 1838 "Trail of Tears," a forced march west, during which thousands of Cherokees died.

Be it enacted by the Senate and House of Representatives of the United States of America, in Congress assembled, That it shall and may be lawful for the President of the United States to cause so much of any territory belonging to the United States, west of the river Mississippi, not included in any state or organized territory, and to which the Indian title has been extinguished, as he may judge necessary, to be divided into a suitable number of districts, for the reception of such tribes or nations of Indians as may choose to exchange the lands where they now reside, and remove there; and to cause each of said districts to be so described by natural or artificial marks, as to be easily distinguished from every other.

Section 2. And be it further enacted, That it shall and may be lawful for the President to exchange any or all of such districts, so to be laid off and described, with any tribe or nation within the limits of any of the states or territories, and with which the United States have existing treaties, for the whole or any part or portion of the territory claimed and occupied by such tribe or nation, within the bounds of any one or more of the states or territories, where the land claimed and occupied by the Indians, is owned by the United States, or the United States are bound to the state within which it lies to extinguish the Indian claim thereto.

Section 3. And be it further enacted, That in the making of any such exchange or exchanges, it shall and may be lawful for the President solemnly to assure the tribe or nation with which the exchange is made, that the United States will forever secure and guaranty to them, and their heirs or successors, the country so exchanged with them; and if they prefer it, that the United States will cause a patent or grant to be made and executed to them for the same: Provided always, That such lands shall revert to the United States, if the Indians become extinct, or abandon the same.

Section 4. And be it further enacted, That if, upon any of the lands now

A grouping of rare Jackson medals, including a Jackson brass clothing button.

As president, Jackson carried out what he believed was the correct government policy toward Native Americans: to separate them from white settlers by forcing them to move west of the Mississippi River. In 1830 he persuaded Congress to pass the Indian Removal Act. Under its provisions, all Indian nations east of the Mississippi River had to exchange their lands for territories west of the river. In 1831, the removal of Native Americans began, as thousands were forced to march hundreds of miles west under conditions of appalling hardship. By the end of Jackson's presidency, there were few Native Americans in the East.

occupied by the Indians, and to be exchanged for, there should be such improvements as add value to the land claimed by any individual or individuals of such tribes or nations, it shall and may be lawful for the President to cause such value to be ascertained by appraisement or otherwise, and to cause such ascertained value to be paid to the person or persons rightfully claiming such improvements. And upon the payment of such valuation, the improvements so valued and paid for, shall pass to the United States, and possession shall not afterwards be permitted to any of the same tribe.

Section 5. And be it further enacted, That upon the making of any such exchange as is contemplated by this act, it shall and may be lawful for the President to cause such aid and assistance to be furnished to the emigrants as may be necessary and proper to enable them to remove to, and settle in, the country for which they may have exchanged; and also, to give them such aid and assistance as may be necessary for their support and subsistence for the first year after their removal.

Section 6. And be it further enacted, That it shall and may be lawful for the President to cause such tribe or nation to be protected, at their new residence, against all interruption or disturbance from any other tribe or nation of Indians, or from any other person or persons whatever.

Section 7. And be it further enacted, That it shall and may be lawful for the President to have the same superintendence and care over any tribe or nation in the country to which they may remove, as contemplated by this act, that he is now authorized to have over them at their present places of residence.

Jackson's Volunteer Toast

The Jefferson Day Dinner held April 13, 1830 at Brown's Indian Queen Hotel in Washington, D.C., was intended to align the Democratic Party with Jeffersonian principles and to celebrate the alliance between the West and the South. President Jackson gave careful thought to the phrasing of his volunteer toast. After listening to 24 prepared speeches, many alluding to state sovereignty and the doctrine of nullification, Jackson delivered the toast on the opposite page. Those present at the dinner described his words as ringing through the banquet hall like one of the former general's battlefield commands.

Our Union: It Must be Preserved

Veto of the Maysville Road Bill

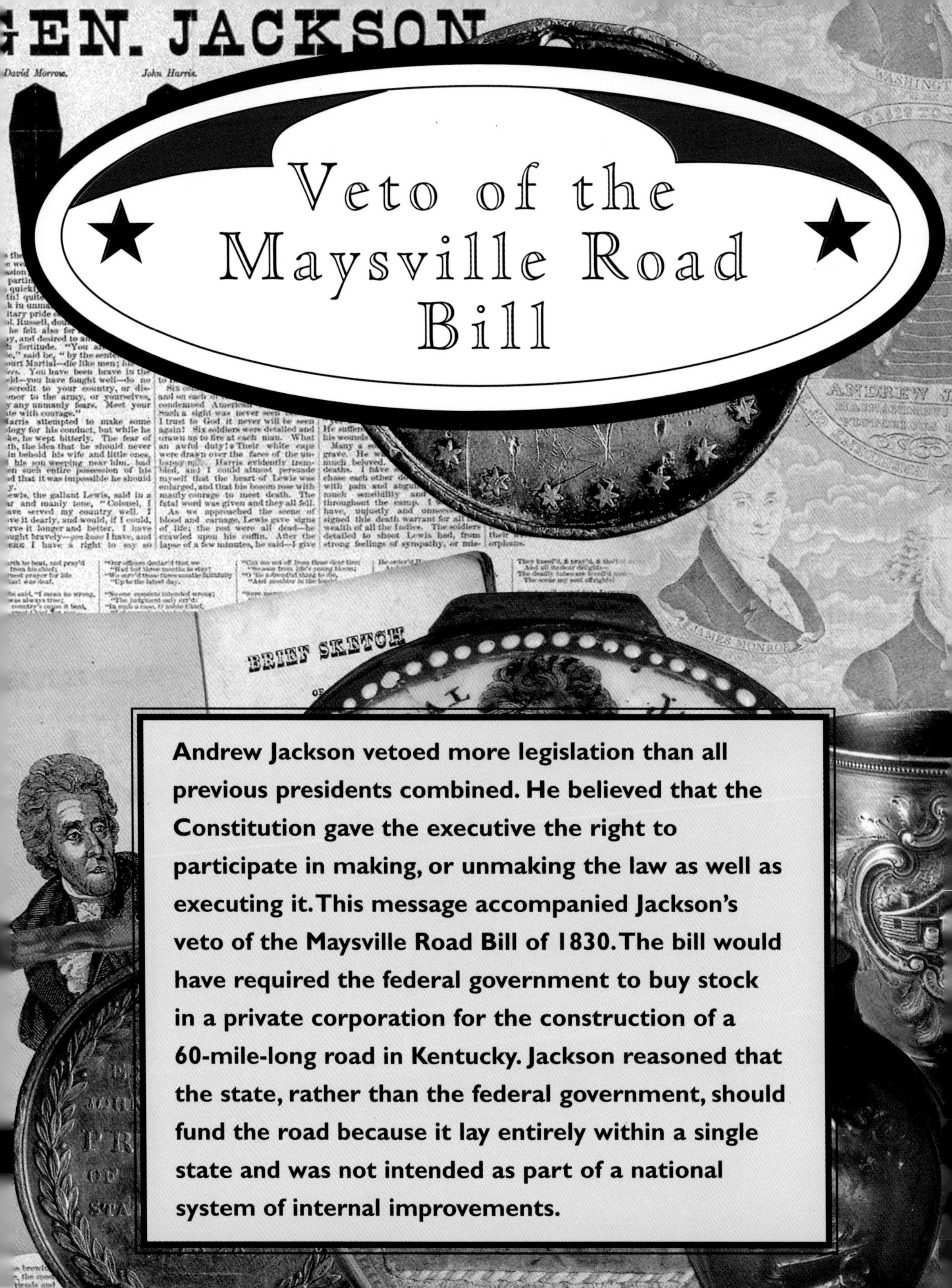

Andrew Jackson vetoed more legislation than all previous presidents combined. He believed that the Constitution gave the executive the right to participate in making, or unmaking the law as well as executing it. This message accompanied Jackson's veto of the Maysville Road Bill of 1830. The bill would have required the federal government to buy stock in a private corporation for the construction of a 60-mile-long road in Kentucky. Jackson reasoned that the state, rather than the federal government, should fund the road because it lay entirely within a single state and was not intended as part of a national system of internal improvements.

I have maturely considered the bill proposing to authorize "a subscription of stock in the Maysville, Washington, Paris, and Lexington Turnpike Road Company," and now return the same to the House of Representatives, in which it originated, with my objections to its passage. [. . .]

The constitutional power of the Federal Government to construct or promote works of internal improvement presents itself in two points of view—the first as bearing upon the sovereignty of the States within whose limits their execution is contemplated, if jurisdiction of the territory which they may occupy be claimed as necessary to their preservation and use; the second as asserting the simple right to appropriate money from the National Treasury in aid of such works when undertaken by State authority, surrendering the claim of jurisdiction. In the first view the question of power is an open one, and can be decided without the embarrassments attending the other, arising from the practice of the government. Although frequently and strenuously attempted, the power to this extent has never been exercised by the Government in a single instance. It does not, in my opinion, possess it; and no bill, therefore, which admits it can receive my official sanction.

But in the other view of the power the question is differently situated. the ground taken at an early period of the Government was "that whenever money has been raised by the general authority and is to be applied to a particular measure, a question arises whether the particular measure be within the enumerated authorities vested in Congress. If it be, the money requisite for it may be applied to it; if not, no such application can be made." The document in which this principle was first advanced is of deservedly high authority, and should be held in grateful remembrance for its immediate agency in rescuing the country from much existing abuse and for its conservative effect upon some of the most valuable principles of the Constitution. The symmetry and purity of the Government would doubtless have been better preserved if this restriction of the power of appropriation could have been maintained without weakening its ability to fulfill the general objects of its institution, an effect so likely to attend its admission, notwithstanding its apparent fitness, that every subsequent Administration of the Government, embracing a period of thirty out of forty-two years of its existence, has adopted a more enlarged construction of the power. It is not my purpose to detain you by a minute recital of the acts which sustain this assertion, but it is proper that I should notice some of the most prominent in order that the reflections which they suggest to my mind may be better understood. [. . .]

The bill before me does not call for a more definite opinion upon the particular circumstances which will warrant appropriations of money by Congress to aid works of internal improvement, for although the extension of the power to apply money beyond that of carrying into effect the object for which it is appropriated has, as we have seen, been long claimed and exercised by the Federal Government, yet such grants have always been professedly under the control of the general principle that the works which might be thus aided should be "of a general, not local, national, not State," character. A disregard of this distinction would of necessity lead to the subversion of the federal system. That even this is an unsafe one, arbitrary in its nature, and liable, consequently, to great abuses, is too obvious to require the confirmation of experience. It is, however, sufficiently definite and imperative to my mind to forbid my approbation of any bill having the character of the one under consideration. I have given to its provisions all the reflection demanded by a just regard for the interests of those of our fellow-citizens who have desired its passage, and by the respect which is due to a coordinate branch of the Government, but I am not able to view it in any other light than as a measure of purely local character; or, if it can be considered national, that no further distinction between the appropriate duties of the General and State

Government used be attempted, for there can be no local interest that may not with equal propriety be denominated national. It has no connection with any established system of improvements; is exclusively within the limits of a State, starting at a point on the Ohio River and running out 60 miles to an interior own, and even as far as the State is interested conferring partial instead of general advantages.

Considering the magnitude and importance of the power, and the embarrassments to which, from the very nature of the thing, its exercise must necessarily be subjected, the real friends of internal improvements ought not to be willing to confide it to accident and chance. [. . .]

In the other view of the subject, and the only remaining one which is my intention to present at this time, is involved the expediency of embarking in a system of internal improvement without a previous amendment of the Constitution explaining and defining the precise powers of the Federal Government over it. Assuming the right to appropriate money to aid in the construction of national works to be warranted by the contemporaneous and continued exposition of the Constitution, its insufficiency for the successful prosecution of them must be admitted by all candid minds. If we look to usage to define the extent of the right, that will be found so variant and embracing so much that has been overruled as to involve the whole subject in great uncertainty and to render the execution of our respective duties in relation to it replete with difficulty and embarrassment. It is in regard to such works and the acquisition of additional territory that the practice obtained its first footing. In most, if not all, other disputed questions of appropriation the construction of the Constitution may be regarded as unsettled if the right to apply money in the enumerated cases is placed on the ground of usage. [. . .]

If it be the desire of the people that the agency of the Federal Government should be confined to the appropriation of money in aid of such undertakings, in virtue of State authorities, then the occasion, the manner, and the extent of the appropriations should be made the subject of constitutional regulation.

This is the more necessary in order that they be equitable among the several States, promote harmony between different sections of the Union and their representatives, preserve other parts of the Constitution from being under-

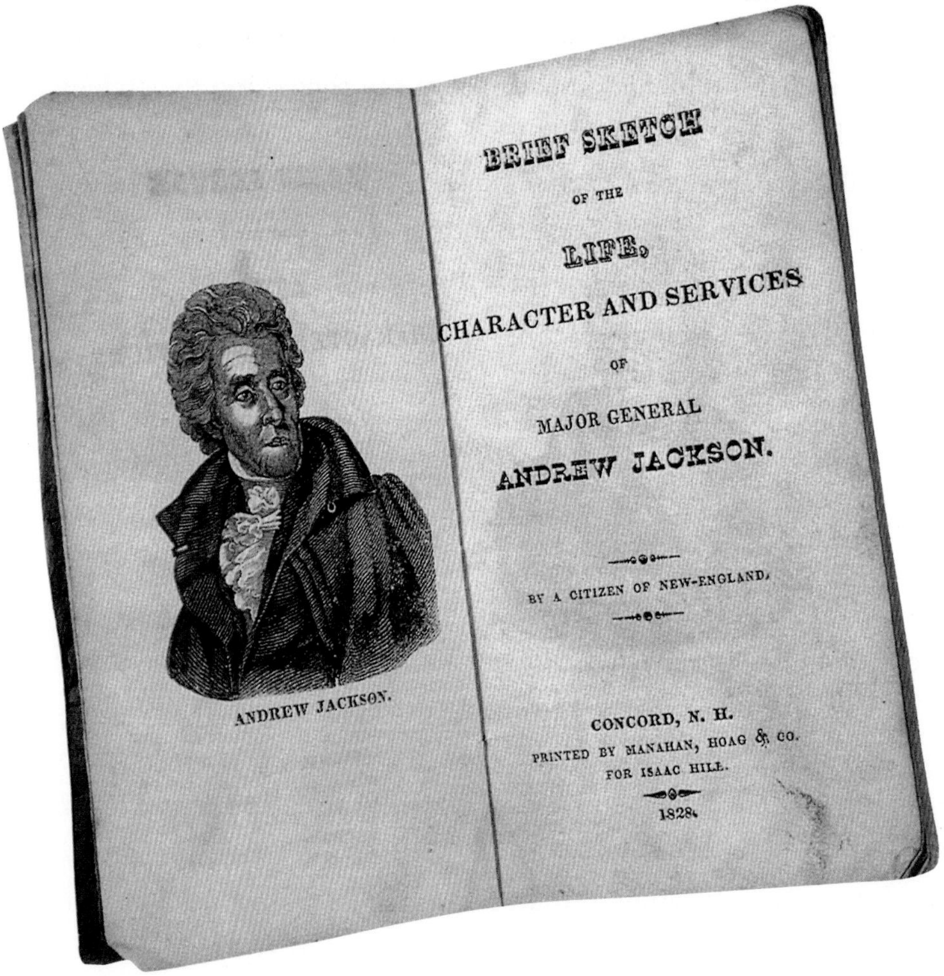

This 1828 Jackson campaign biography was written "by a citizen of New England." "Campaign literature" is the term used to describe all varieties of material circulated during a political campaign to influence the voter. This includes biographies of the candidates, pamphlets on specific campaign issues, campaign songs, posters, and campaign books which usually contained statistical data, documents, arguments, and other such material.

mined by the exercise of doubtful powers or the too great extension of those which are not so, and protect the whole subject against the deleterious influence of combinations to carry by concert measures which, considered by themselves, might meet but little countenance.

That a Constitutional adjustment of this power upon equitable principles is in the highest degree desirable can scarcely be doubted, nor can it fail to be promoted by every sincere friend to the success of our political institutions. In no government are appeals to the source of power in cases of real doubt more suitable than in ours. No good motive can be assigned for the exercise of power by the constituted authorities, while those for whose benefit it is to be exercised have not conferred it and may not be willing to confer it. It would seem to me that an honest application of the conceded powers of the General Government to the advancement of the common weal present a sufficient scope to satisfy a reasonable ambition. The difficulty and supposed impracticability of obtaining an amendment of the Constitution in this respect is, I firmly believe, in a great degree unfounded. The time has never yet been when the patriotism and intelligence of the American people were not fully equal to the greatest exigency, and it never will when the subject calling forth their interposition is plainly presented to them. To do so with the questions involved in this bill, and to urge them to an early, zealous, and full consideration of their deep importance, is, in my estimation, among the highest of our duties. [. . .]

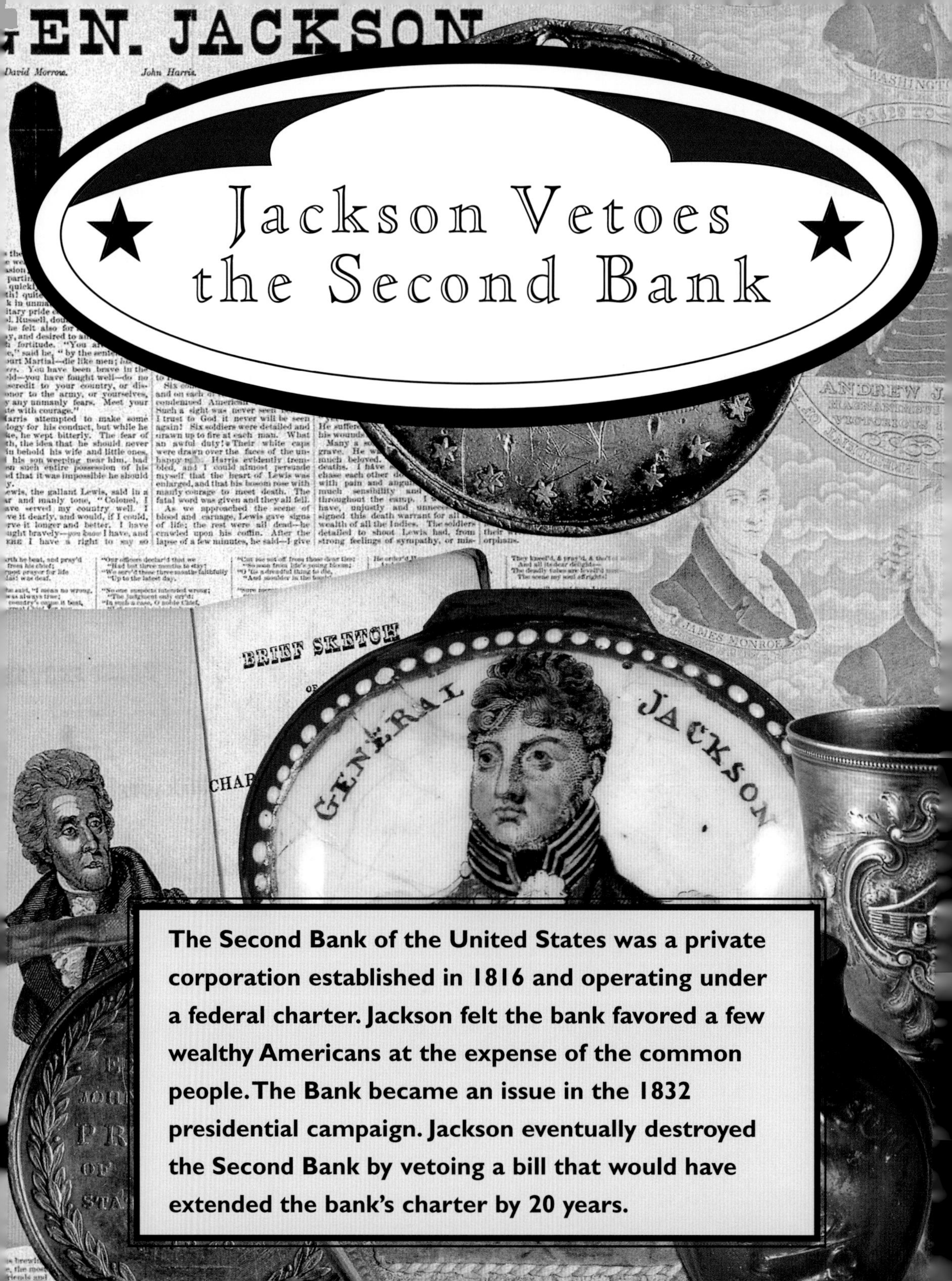

Jackson Vetoes the Second Bank

The Second Bank of the United States was a private corporation established in 1816 and operating under a federal charter. Jackson felt the bank favored a few wealthy Americans at the expense of the common people. The Bank became an issue in the 1832 presidential campaign. Jackson eventually destroyed the Second Bank by vetoing a bill that would have extended the bank's charter by 20 years.

The bill "to modify and continue" the act entitled "An act to incorporate the subscribers to the Bank of the United States" was presented to me on the 4th July instant. Having considered it with that solemn regard to the principles of the Constitution which the day was calculated to inspire, and come to the conclusion that it ought not to become a law, I herewith return it to the Senate, in which it originated, with my objections.

A bank of the United States is in many respects convenient for the Government and useful to the people. Entertaining this opinion, and deeply impressed with the belief that some of the powers and privileges possessed by the existing bank are unauthorized by the Constitution, subversive of the rights of the States, and dangerous to the liberties of the people, I felt it my duty at an early period of my Administration to call the attention of Congress to the practicability of organizing an institution combining all its advantages and obviating these objections. I sincerely regret that in the act before me I can perceive none of those modifications of the bank charter which are necessary, in my opinion, to make it compatible with justice, with sound policy, or with the Constitution of our country.

The present corporate body, denominated the president, directors, and company of the Bank of the United States, will have existed at the time this act is intended to take effect twenty years. It enjoys an exclusive privilege of banking under the authority of the General Government, a monopoly of its favor and support, and, as a necessary consequence, almost a monopoly of the foreign and domestic exchange. The powers, privileges, and favors bestowed upon it in the original charter, by increasing the value of the stock far above its par value, operated as a gratuity of many millions to the stockholders.

An apology may be found for the failure to guard against this result in the consideration that the effect of the original act of incorporation could not be certainly foreseen at the time of its passage. The act before me proposes another gratuity to the holders of the same stock, and in many cases to the same men, of at least seven millions more. This donation finds no apology in any uncertainty as to the effect of the act. On all hands it is conceded that its passage will increase at least 20 or 30 percent more the market price of the stock, subject to the payment of the annuity of $200,000 per year secured by the act, thus adding in a moment one-fourth to its par value. It is not our own citizens only who are to receive the bounty of our Government. More than eight millions of the stock of this bank are held by foreigners. By this act the American Republic proposes virtually to make them a present of some millions of dollars. For these gratuities to foreigners and to some of our own opulent citizens the act secures no equivalent whatever. They are the certain gains of the present stockholders under the operation of this act, after making full allowance for the payment of the bonus.

Every monopoly and all exclusive privileges are granted at the expense of the public, which ought to receive a fair equivalent. The many millions which this act proposes to bestow on the stockholders of the existing bank must come directly or indirectly out of the earnings of the American people. It is due to them, therefore, if their Government sell monopolies and exclusive privileges, that they should at least exact for them as much as they are worth in open market. The value of the monopoly in this case may be correctly ascertained. The twenty-eight millions of stock would probably be at an advance of 50 per cent, and command in market at least $42,000,000, subject to the payment of the present bonus. The present value of the monopoly, therefore, is $17,000,000, and this the act proposes to sell for three millions, payable in fifteen annual installments of $200,000 each.

It is not conceivable how the present stockholders can have any claim to the special favor of the Government. The present corporation has enjoyed its monopoly during the period stipulated in the original contract. If we must have such a corporation, why should not the Government sell out the whole stock and thus secure to the people the full market value of the privileges

granted? Why should not Congress create and sell twenty-eight millions of stock, incorporating the purchasers with all the powers and privileges secured in this act and putting the premium upon the sales into the Treasury?

But this act does not permit competition in the purchase of this monopoly. It seems to be predicated on the erroneous idea that the present stockholders have a prescriptive right not only to the favor but to the bounty of Government. It appears that more than a fourth part of the stock is held by foreigners and the residue is held by a few hundred of our own citizens, chiefly of the richest class. For their benefit does this act exclude the whole American people from competition in the purchase of this monopoly and dispose of it for many millions less than it is worth. This seems the less excusable because some of our citizens not now stockholders petitioned that the door of competition might be opened, and offered to take a charter on terms much more favorable to the Government and country.

But this proposition, although made by men whose aggregate wealth is believed to be equal to all the private stock in the existing bank, has been set aside, and the bounty of our Government is proposed to be again bestowed on the few who have been fortunate enough to secure the stock and at this moment wield the power of the existing institution. I can not perceive the justice or policy of this course. If our Government must sell monopolies, it would seem to be its duty to take nothing less than their full value, and if gratuities must be made once in fifteen or twenty years let them not be bestowed on the subjects of a foreign government nor upon a designated and favored class of men in our own country. It is but justice and good policy, as far as the nature of the case will admit, to confine our favors to our own fellow-citizens, and let each in his turn enjoy an opportunity to profit by our bounty. In the bearings of the act before me upon these points I find ample reasons why it should not become a law.

It has been urged as an argument in favor of rechartering the present bank that the calling in its loans will produce great embarrassment and distress. The time allowed to close its concerns is ample, and if it has been well managed its pressure will be light, and heavy only in case its management has been bad. If, therefore, it shall produce distress, the fault will be its own, and it would furnish a reason against renewing a power which has been so obviously abused. But will there ever be a time when this reason will be less powerful? To acknowledge its force is to admit that the bank ought to be perpetual, and as a consequence the present stockholders and those inheriting their rights as successors be established a privileged order, clothed both with great political power and enjoying immense pecuniary advantages from their connection with the Government.

The modifications of the existing charter proposed by this act are not such, in my view, as make it consistent with the rights of the States or the liberties of the people. The qualification of the right of the bank to hold real estate, the limitation of its power to establish branches, and the power reserved to Congress to forbid the circulation of small notes are restrictions comparatively of little value or importance. All the objectionable principles of the existing corporation, and most of its odious features, are retained without alleviation. [. . .]

If we must have a bank with private stockholders, every consideration of sound policy and every impulse of American feeling admonishes that it should be purely American. Its stockholders should be composed exclusively of our own citizens, who at least ought to be friendly to our Government and willing to support it in times of difficulty and danger. So abundant is domestic capital that competition in subscribing for the stock of local banks has recently led almost to riots. To a bank exclusively of American stockholders, possessing the powers and privileges granted by this act, subscriptions for $200,000,000 could be readily obtained. Instead of sending abroad the stock of the bank in which the Government must deposit its funds and on which it must rely to sustain its credit in times of emergency, it would rather seem to be expedient to prohibit its sale to aliens under penalty of absolute forfeiture.

It is maintained by the advocates of the bank that its constitutionality in all its features ought to be considered as settled by precedent and by the decision of the Supreme Court. To this conclusion I can not assent. Mere precedent is a dangerous source of authority, and should not be regarded as deciding questions of constitutional power except where the acquiescence of the people and the States can be considered as well settled. So far from this being the case on this subject, an argument against the bank might be based on precedent. One Congress, in 1791, decided in favor of a bank; another, in 1811, decided against it. One Congress, in 1815, decided against a bank; another, in 1816, decided in its favor. Prior to the present Congress, therefore, the precedents drawn from that source were equal. If we resort to the States, the expressions of legislative, judicial, and executive opinions against the bank have been probably to those in its favor as 4 to 1. There is nothing in prece-

Real and serious financial issues were involved in the rechartering of the Second Bank of the United States. Jackson's opposition came as much from what the Bank symbolized as from what it actually did. Many of the political developments of the 1830s had the same symbolic quality.

The item on the right is a paper-mâché snuffbox with a picture of Jackson. The paper transfer portrait was sealed with several coats of lacquer.

dent, therefore, which, if its authority were admitted, ought to weigh in favor of the act before me. [. . .]

On two subjects only does the Constitution recognize in Congress the power to grant exclusive privileges or monopolies. It declares that "Congress shall have power to promote the progress of science and useful arts by securing for limited times to authors and inventors the exclusive right to their respective writings and discoveries." Out of this express delegation of power have grown our laws of patents and copyrights. As the Constitution expressly delegates to Congress the power to grant exclusive privileges in these cases as the means of executing the substantive power "to promote the progress of science and useful arts," it is consistent with the fair rules of construction to conclude that such a power was not intended to be granted as a means of accomplishing any other end. On every other subject which comes within the scope of Congressional power there is an ever-living discretion in the use of proper means, which can not be restricted or abolished without an amendment of the Constitution. Every act of Congress, therefore, which attempts by grants of monopolies or sale of exclusive privileges for a limited time, or a time without limit, to restrict or extinguish its own discretion in the choice of means to execute its delegated powers is equivalent to a legislative amendment of the Constitution, and palpably unconstitutional.

This act authorizes and encourages transfers of its stock to foreigners and grants them an exemption from all State and national taxation. So far from being "necessary and proper" that the bank should possess this power to make it a safe and efficient agent of the Government in its fiscal operations, it is calculated to convert the Bank of the United States into a foreign bank, to impoverish our people in time of peace, to disseminate a foreign influence through every section of the Republic, and in war to endanger our independence.

The several States reserved the power at the formation of the Constitution to regulate and control titles and transfers of real property, and most, if not all, of them have laws disqualifying aliens from acquiring or holding lands

within their limits. But this act, in disregard of the undoubted right of the States to prescribe such disqualifications, gives to aliens stockholders in this bank an interest and title, as members of the corporation, to all the real property it may acquire within any of the States of this Union. This privilege granted to aliens is not "necessary" to enable the bank to perform its public duties, nor in any sense "proper," because it is vitally subversive of the rights of the States.

The Government of the United States have no constitutional power to purchase lands within the States except "for the erection of forts, magazines, arsenals, dockyards, and other needful buildings," and even for these objects only "by the consent of the legislature of the State in which the same shall be." By making themselves stockholders in the bank and granting to the corporation the power to purchase lands for other purposes they assume a power not granted in the Constitution and grant to others what they do not themselves possess. It is not necessary to the receiving, safe-keeping, or transmission of the funds of the Government that the bank should possess this power, and it is not proper that Congress should thus enlarge the powers delegated to them in the Constitution.

The old Bank of the United States possessed a capital of only $11,000,000, which was found fully sufficient to enable it with dispatch and safety to perform all the functions required of it by the Government. The capital of the present bank is $35,000,000—at least twenty-four millions more than experience has proved to be necessary to enable a bank to perform its public functions. The public debt which existed during the period of the old bank and on the establishment of the new has been nearly paid off, and our revenue will soon be reduced. This increase of capital is therefore not for public but for private purposes.

The Government is the only "proper" judge where its agents should reside and keep their offices, because it best knows where their presence will be "necessary." It can not, therefore, be "necessary" or "proper" to authorize the bank to locate branches where it pleases to perform the public service, without consulting the Government, and contrary to its will. The principle laid down by the Supreme Court concedes that Congress can not establish a bank for purposes of private speculation and gain, but only as a means of executing the delegated powers of the General Government. By the same principle a branch bank can not constitutionally be established for other than public purposes. The power which this act gives to establish two branches in any State, without the injunction or request of the Government and for other than public purposes, is not "necessary" to the due execution of the powers delegated to Congress. [. . .]

It is to be regretted that the rich and powerful too often bend the acts of government to their selfish purposes. Distinctions in society will always exist under every just government. Equality of talents, of education, or of wealth can not be produced by human institutions. In the full enjoyment of the gifts of Heaven and the fruits of superior industry, economy, and virtue, every man is equally entitled to protection by law; but when the laws undertake to add to these natural and just advantages artificial distinctions, to grant titles, gratuities, and exclusive privileges, to make the rich richer and the potent more powerful, the humble members of society—the farmers, mechanics, and laborers—who have neither the time nor the means of securing like favors to themselves, have a right to complain of the injustice of their Government. There are no necessary evils in government. Its evils exist only in its abuses. If it would confine itself to equal protection, and, as Heaven does its rains, shower its favors alike on the high and the low, the rich and the poor, it would be an unqualified blessing. In the act before me there seems to be a wide and unnecessary departure from these just principles.

Nor is our Government to be maintained or our Union preserved by invasions of the rights and powers of the several States. In thus attempting to make our General Government strong we make it weak. Its true strength consists in leaving individuals and States as much as possible to themselves—

in making itself felt, not in its power, but in its beneficence; not in its control, but in its protection; not in binding the States more closely to the center, but leaving each to move unobstructed in its proper orbit.

Experience should teach us wisdom. Most of the difficulties our Government now encounters and most of the dangers which impend over our Union have sprung from an abandonment of the legitimate objects of Government by our national legislation, and the adoption of such principles as are embodied in this act. Many of our rich men have not been content with equal protection and equal benefits, but have besought us to make them richer by act of Congress. By attempting to gratify their desires we have in the results of our legislation arrayed section against section, interest against interest, and man against man, in a fearful commotion which threatens to shake the foundations of our Union. It is time to pause in our career to review our principles, and if possible revive that devoted patriotism and spirit of compromise which distinguished the sages of the Revolution and the fathers of our Union. If we can not at once, in justice to interests vested under improvident legislation, make our Government what it ought to be, we can at least take a stand against all new grants of monopolies and exclusive privileges, against any prostitution of our Government to the advancement of the few at the expense of the many, and in favor of compromise and gradual reform in our code of laws and system of political economy.

I have now done my duty to my country. If sustained by my fellow citizens, I shall be grateful and happy; if not, I shall find in the motives which impel me ample grounds for contentment and peace. In the difficulties which surround us and the dangers which threaten our institutions there is cause for neither dismay nor alarm. For relief and deliverance let us firmly rely on that kind Providence which I am sure watches with peculiar care over the destinies of our Republic, and on the intelligence and wisdom of our countrymen. Through His abundant goodness and heir patriotic devotion our liberty and Union will be preserved.

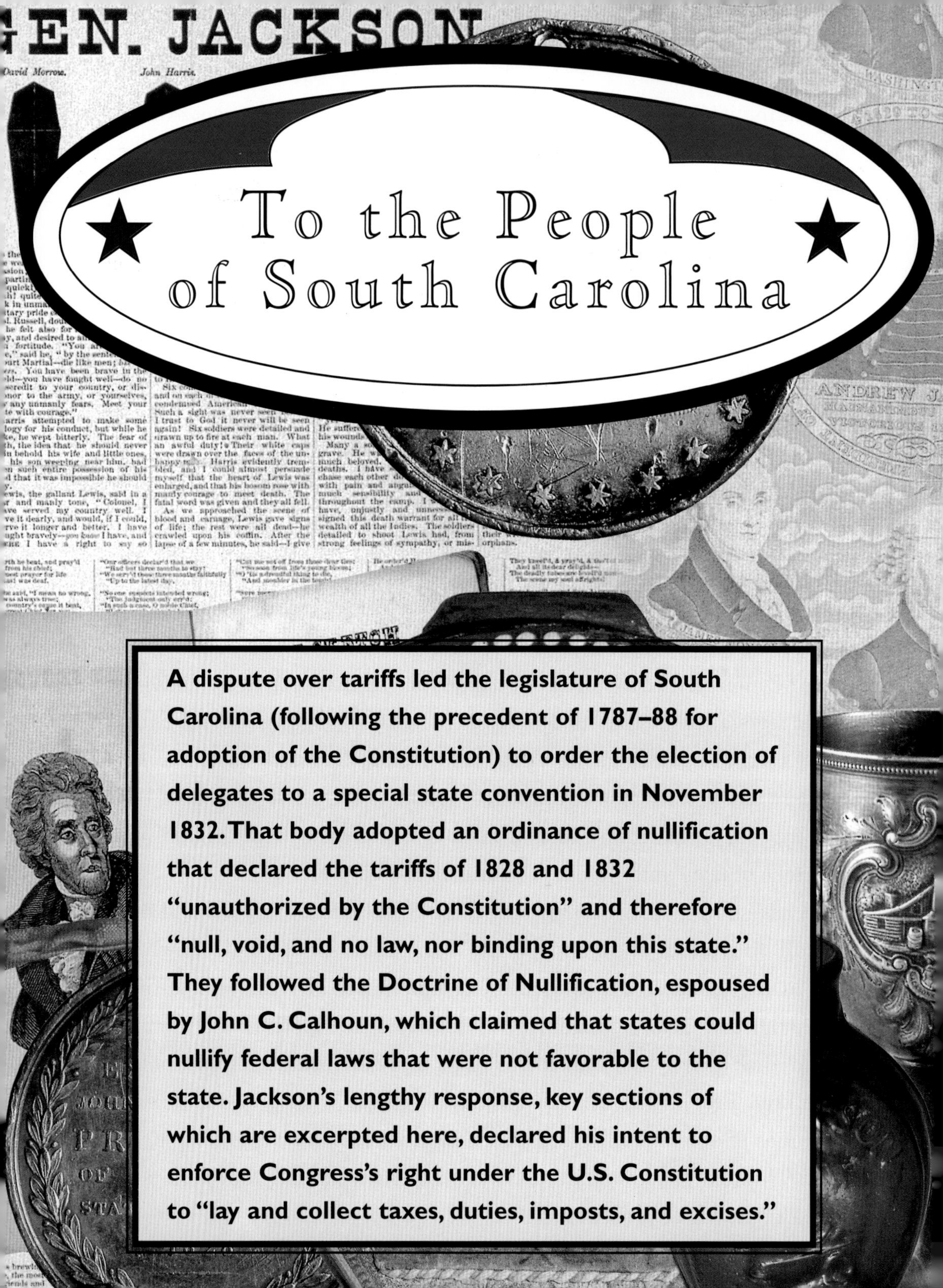

To the People of South Carolina

A dispute over tariffs led the legislature of South Carolina (following the precedent of 1787–88 for adoption of the Constitution) to order the election of delegates to a special state convention in November 1832. That body adopted an ordinance of nullification that declared the tariffs of 1828 and 1832 "unauthorized by the Constitution" and therefore "null, void, and no law, nor binding upon this state." They followed the Doctrine of Nullification, espoused by John C. Calhoun, which claimed that states could nullify federal laws that were not favorable to the state. Jackson's lengthy response, key sections of which are excerpted here, declared his intent to enforce Congress's right under the U.S. Constitution to "lay and collect taxes, duties, imposts, and excises."

Whereas a convention assembled in the State of South Carolina have passed an ordinance by which they declare "that the several acts and parts of acts of the Congress of the United States purporting to be laws for the imposting of duties and imposts on the importation of foreign commodities, . . . are unauthorized by the Constitution of the United States, and violate the true meaning and intent thereof, and are null and void and no law," nor binding on the citizens of that State or its officers; and by the said ordinance it is further declared to be unlawful for any of the constituted authorities of the State or of the United States to enforce the payment of the duties imposed by the said acts within the same State, and that it is duty of the legislature to pass such laws as may be necessary to give full effect to the said ordinance; and

Whereas by the said ordinance it is further ordained that in no case of law or equity decided in the courts of said State wherein shall be drawn in question the validity of the said ordinance, or of the acts of the legislature that may be passed to give it effect, or of the said laws of the United States, no appeal shall be allowed to the Supreme Court of the United States, nor shall any copy of the record be permitted or allowed for that purpose, and that any person attempting to take such appeal shall be punished as for contempt of court; and [. . .]

Whereas the said ordinance prescribes to the people of South Carolina a course of conduct in direct violation of their duty as citizens of the United States, contrary to the laws of their country, subversive of its Constitution, and having for its object the destruction of the Union—

To preserve this bond of our political existence from destruction, to maintain inviolate this state of national honor and prosperity, and to justify the confidence my fellow-citizens have reposed in me, I, Andrew Jackson, President of the United States, have thought proper to issue this my proclamation, stating my views of the Constitution and laws applicable to the measures adopted by the convention of South Carolina and to the reasons they have put forth to sustain them, declaring the course which duty will require me to pursue, and, appealing to the understanding and patriotism of the people, warn them of the consequences that must inevitably result from an observance of the dictates of the convention. [. . .]

The ordinance is founded, not on the indefeasible right of resisting acts which are plainly unconstitutional and too oppressive to be endured, but on the strange position that any one State may not only declare an act of Congress void, but prohibit its execution; that they may do this consistently with the Constitution; that the true construction of that instrument permits a State to retain its place in the Union and yet be bound by no other of its laws than those it may choose to consider as constitutional. It is true, they add, that to justify this abrogation of a law it must be palpably contrary to the Constitution; but it is evident that to give the right of resisting laws of that description, coupled with the uncontrolled right to decide what laws deserve that character, is to give the power of resisting all laws; for as by the theory there is no appeal, the reasons alleged by the State, good or bad, must prevail. If it should be said that public opinion is a sufficient check against the abuse of this power, it may be asked why it is not deemed a sufficient guard against the passage of an unconstitutional act by Congress? There is, however, a restraint in this last case, which makes the assumed power of a State more indefensible, and which does not exist in the other. There are two appeals from an unconstitutional act passed by Congress—one to the Judiciary, the other to the people and the States. There is no appeal from the State decision in theory, and the practical illustration shows that the courts are closed against an application to review it, both judges and jurors being sworn to decide in its favor. But reasoning on this subject is superfluous, when our social compact, in express terms, declares that the laws of the United States, its Constitution, and treaties made under it, are the supreme law of the land; and, for greater caution, adds "that the judges in every State shall be bound thereby, anything

in the Constitution or laws of any State to the contrary notwithstanding." And it may be asserted without fear of refutation, that no Federative Government could exist without a similar provision. Look for a moment to the consequence. If South Carolina considers the revenue laws unconstitutional, and has a right to prevent their execution in the port of Charleston, there would be a clear constitutional objection to their collection in every other port, and no revenue could be collected any where; for all imposts must be equal. It is no answer to repeat, that an unconstitutional law is no law, so long as the question of its legality is to be decided by the State itself; for every law operating injuriously upon any local interest will be perhaps thought, and certainly represented, as unconstitutional, and, as has been shown,there is no appeal.

If this doctrine had been established at an earlier day, the Union would have been dissolved in its infancy. The excise law in Pennsylvania, the embargo and nonintercourse law in the Eastern States, the carriage tax in Virginia, were all deemed unconstitutional, and were more unequal in their operation than any of the laws now complained of; but, fortunately, none of those States discovered that they had the right now claimed by South Carolina. The war into which we were forced to support the dignity of the nation and the rights of our citizens might have ended in defeat and disgrace, instead of victory and honor, if the States who supposed it a ruinous and unconstitutional measure had thought they possessed the right of nullifying the act by which it was declared and denying supplies for its prosecution. Hardly and unequally as those measures bore upon several members of the Union, to the legislatures of none did this efficient and peaceable remedy, as it is called, suggest itself. The discovery of this important feature in our Constitution was reserved to the present day. To the statesmen of South Carolina belongs the invention, and upon the citizens of that State will unfortunately fall the evils of reducing it to practice.

If the doctrine of a State veto upon the laws of the Union carries with it internal evidence of its impracticable absurdity, our constitutional history will also afford abundant proof that it would have been repudiated with indignation had it been proposed to form a feature in our Government.

Our present Constitution was formed [. . .] in vain if this fatal doctrine prevails. It was formed for important objects that are announced in the preamble, made in the name and by the authority of the people of the United States, whose delegates framed and whose conventions approved it. The most important among these objects—that which is placed first in rank, on which all the others rest—is "*to form a more perfect union.*" Now, is it possible that even if there were no express provision giving supremacy to the Constitution and laws of the United States over those of the states, can it be conceived that an instrument made for the purpose of "*forming a more perfect union*" than that of the Confederation could be so constructed by the assembled wisdom of our country as to substitute for that Confederation a form of government dependent for its existence on the local interest, the party spirit, of a State, or of a prevailing faction in a State? Even man of plain, unsophisticated understanding who hears the question will give such an answer as will preserve the Union. Metaphysical subtlety, in pursuit of an impracticable theory, could alone have devised one that is calculated to destroy it.

I consider, then, the power to annul a law of the United States, assumed by one State, *incompatible with the existence of the Union, contradicted expressly by the letter of the Constitution, unauthorized by its spirit, inconsistent with every principle on which it was founded, and destructive of the great object for which it was formed.*

After this general view of the leading principle, we must examine the particular application of it which is made in the ordinance.

The Preamble rests its justification on these grounds: It assumes as a fact that the obnoxious laws, although they purport to be laws for raising revenue, were in reality intended for the protection of manufactures, which purpose it asserts to be unconstitutional; that the operation of these laws is unequal; that the amount raised by them is greater than is required by the wants of the

An 1828 political broadside. John C. Calhoun was a congressman, secretary of war, and seventh vice president (1825–32) of the United States. Calhoun was elected vice president under John Quincy Adams in 1824 and was reelected under Andrew Jackson in 1828. By the early 1830s, Calhoun became as extremely devoted to nullification as he had been to nationalism earlier in his career. Each state was sovereign, Calhoun argued. And, the Constitution of the United States was an agreement among sovereign states. Therefore, any one state, but not the Supreme Court of the United States, could declare an act of Congress unconstitutional. The supporters of such an act could override the nullified act by an amendment to the Constitution—which requires a two-thirds vote in each house of Congress and the approval of three-fourths of the states.

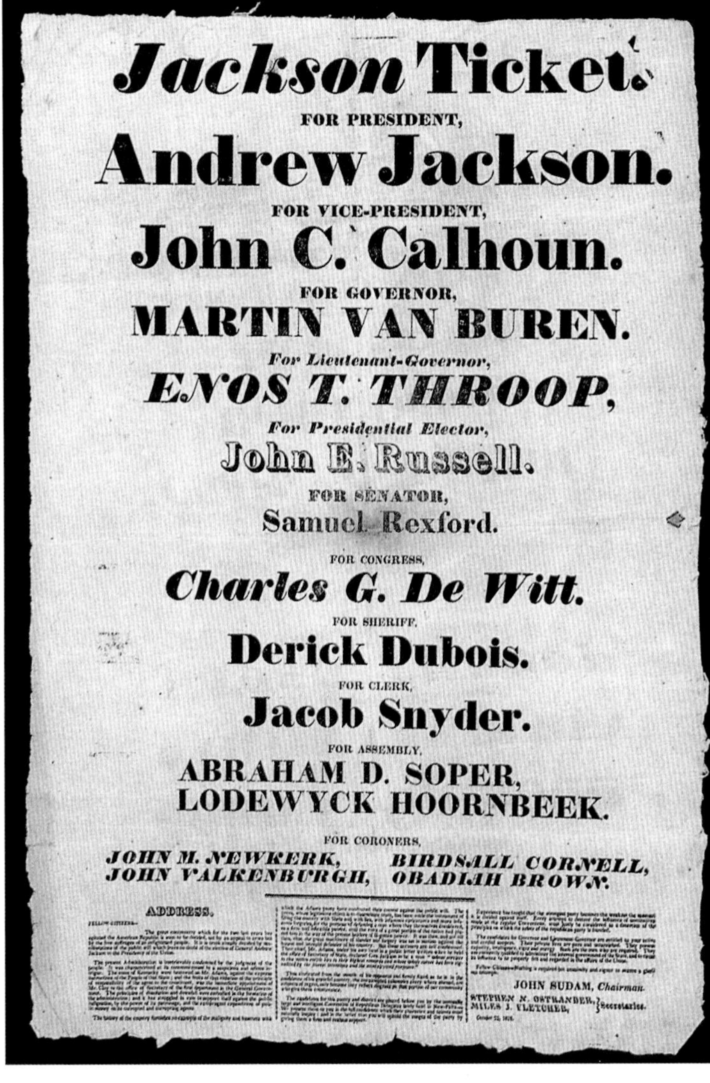

Jackson Ticket.

FOR PRESIDENT,

Andrew Jackson.

FOR VICE-PRESIDENT,

John C. Calhoun.

FOR GOVERNOR,

MARTIN VAN BUREN.

For Lieutenant-Governor,

ENOS T. THROOP,

For Presidential Elector,

John E. Russell.

FOR SENATOR,

Samuel Rexford.

FOR CONGRESS,

Charles G. De Witt.

FOR SHERIFF,

Derick Dubois.

FOR CLERK,

Jacob Snyder.

FOR ASSEMBLY,

ABRAHAM D. SOPER,
LODEWYCK HOORNBEEK.

FOR CORONERS,

JOHN M. NEWKERK, BIRDSALL CORNELL,
JOHN VALKENBURGH, OBADIAH BROWN.

ADDRESS.

JOHN SUDAM, *Chairman.*

government; and, finally, that the proceeds are to be applied to objects unauthorized by the Constitution. These are the only causes alleged to justify an open opposition to the laws of the country and a threat of seceding from the Union if any attempt should be made to enforce them. The first virtually acknowledges that the law in question was passed under a power expressly given by the Constitution to lay and collect imposts; but its constitutionality is drawn in question from the *motives* of those who passed it. However apparent this purpose may he in the present case, nothing can be more dangerous than to admit the position that an unconstitutional purpose entertained by the members who assent to a law enacted under a constitutional power shall make that law void. For how is that purpose to be ascertained? Who is to make the scrutiny? How often may bad purposes be falsely imputed, in how many cases are they concealed by false professions, in how many is no declaration of motive made? Admit this doctrine, and you give to the States an uncontrolled right to decide, and every law may be annulled under this pretext. If, therefore, the absurd and dangerous doctrine should be admitted that a State may annul an unconstitutional law, or one that it deems such, it will not apply to the present case.

The next objection is that the laws in question operate unequally. This objection may be made with truth to every law that has been or can be passed. The wisdom of man never yet contrived a system of taxation that would operate with perfect equality. If the unequal operation of a law makes it unconstitutional, and if all laws of that description may be abrogated by any State for that cause, then, indeed, is the Federal Constitution unworthy of the slightest effort for its presentation. [. . .]

Nor did the States, when they severally ratified it, do so under the impression that a veto on the laws of the United States was reserved to them or that they could exercise it by implication. Search the debates in all their conventions, examine the speeches of the most zealous opposers of federal authority, look at the amendments that were proposed; they are all silent—not a syllable uttered, not a vote given, not a motion made to correct the explicit supremacy given to the laws of the Union over those of the states, or to show that implication, as is now contended, could defeat it. No; we have not erred. The Constitution is still the object of our reverence, the bond of our Union, our defense in danger, the source of our prosperity in peace. It shall descend, as we have received it, uncorrupted by sophistical construction, to our posterity; and

the sacrifices of local interests, of State prejudices, of personal animosities that were made to bring it into existence will again be patriotically offered for its support.

The two remaining objections made by the ordinance to these laws are that the sums intended to be raised by them are greater than are required, and that the proceeds will be unconstitutionally employed. [. . .]

The ordinance, with the same knowledge of the future that characterizes a former objection, tells you that the proceeds of the tax will be unconstitutionally applied. If this could be ascertained with certainty, the objection would with more propriety be reserved for the law so applying the proceeds, but surely cannot be urged against the laws levying the duty.

These are the allegations contained in the ordinance. Examine them seriously, my fellow citizens; judge for yourselves. I appeal to you to determine whether they are so clear, so convincing, as to leave no doubt of their correctness; and even if you should come to this conclusion, how far they justify the reckless, destructive course which you are directed to pursue. Review these objections and the conclusions drawn from them once more. What are they? Every law, then, for raising revenue, according to the South Carolina ordinance, may be rightfully annulled, unless it be so framed as no law ever will or can be framed. Congress has a right to pass laws for raising revenue and each State has a right to oppose their execution—two rights directly opposed to each other; and yet is this absurdity supposed to be contained in an instrument drawn for the express purpose of avoiding collisions between the States and the General Government by an assembly of the most enlightened statesmen and purest patriots ever embodied for a similar purpose.

In vain have these sages declared that Congress shall have power to lay and collect taxes, duties, imposts, and excises; in vain have they provided that they shall have power to pass laws which shall be necessary and proper to carry those powers into execution, that those laws and that Constitution shall be the "supreme law of the land, and that the judges in every State shall be bound thereby, anything in the constitution or laws of any State to the contrary notwithstanding" [. . .] if a bare majority of the voters in any one State may, on a real or supposed knowledge of the intent with which a law has been passed, declare themselves free from its operation; [. . .]

The Constitution declares that the judicial powers of the United States extend to cases arising under the laws of the United States, and that such laws, the Constitution, and treaties shall be paramount to the State constitutions and laws. The judiciary act prescribes the mode by which the case may be brought before a court of the United States by appeal when a State tribunal shall decide against this provision of the Constitution. The ordinance declares there shall be no appeal—makes the State law paramount to the Constitution and laws of the United States, forces judges and jurors to swear that they will disregard their provisions, and even makes it penal in a suitor to attempt relief by appeal. It further declares that it shall not be lawful for the authorities of the United States or of that State to enforce the payment of duties imposed by the revenue laws within its limits.

Here is a law of the United States, not even pretended to be unconstitutional, repealed by the authority of a small majority of the voters of a single State. Here is a provision of the Constitution which is solemnly abrogated by the same authority.

On such expositions and reasonings the ordinance grounds not only an assertion of the right to annul the laws of which it complains but to enforce it by a threat of seceding from the Union if any attempt is made to execute them.

This right to secede is deduced from the nature of the Constitution, which, they say, is a compact between sovereign States who have preserved their whole sovereignty and therefore are subject to no superior; that because they made the compact they can break it when in their opinion it has been departed from by the other States. Fallacious as this course of reasoning is, it enlists State pride and finds advocates in the honest prejudices of those who have not studied the nature of our government sufficiently to see the radical error on which it rests. [. . .]

The Constitution of the United States, then, forms a *government*, not a league; and whether it be formed by compact between the States or in any other manner, its character is the same. It is a Government in which all the people are represented, which operates directly on the people individually, not upon the States; they retained all the power they did not grant. But each State, having expressly parted with so many powers as to constitute, jointly with the other States, a single nation, cannot, from that period, possess any right to secede, because such secession does not break a league but destroys the unity of a nation; and any injury to that unity is not only a breach which would result from the contravention of a compact but it is an offense against the whole Union.

To say that any State may at pleasure secede from the Union is to say that the United States are not a nation, because it would be a solecism to contend that any part of a nation might dissolve its connection with the other parts, to their injury or ruin, without committing any offense. Secession, like any other revolutionary act, may be morally justified by the extremity of oppression; but to call it a constitutional right is confounding the meaning of terms, and can only be done through gross error or to deceive those who are willing to assert a right, but would pause before they made a revolution or incur the penalties consequent on a failure.

Because the Union was formed by a compact, it is said the parties to that compact may, when they feel themselves aggrieved, depart from it; but it is precisely because it is a compact that they cannot. A compact is an agreement or binding obligation. It may by its terms have a sanction or penalty for its breach, or it may not. If it contains no sanction, it may be broken with no other consequence than moral guilt; if it have a sanction, then the breach incurs the designated or implied penalty. A league between independent nations generally has no sanction other than a moral one; or if it should contain a penalty, as there is no common superior it cannot be enforced. A government, on the contrary, always has a sanction, express or implied; and in our case it is both necessarily implied and expressly given. An attempt by force of arms to destroy a government is an offense, by whatever means the constitutional compact may have been formed; and such government has the right by the law of self-defense to pass acts for punishing the offender, unless that right is modified, restrained, or resumed by the constitutional act. In our system, although it is modified in the case of treason, yet authority is expressly given to pass all laws necessary to carry its powers into effect, and under this grant provision has been made for punishing acts which obstruct the due administration of the laws.

It would seem superfluous to add anything to show the nature of that Union which connects us, but as erroneous opinions on this subject are the foundation of doctrines the most destructive to our peace, I must give some further development to my views on this subject. [. . .]

The States severally have not retained their entire sovereignty. It has been shown that in becoming parts of a nation, not members of a league, they surrendered many of their essential parts of sovereignty. The right to make treaties, declare war, levy taxes, exercise exclusive judicial and legislative powers were all of them functions of sovereign power. The States, then, for all these important purposes, were no longer sovereign. The allegiance of their citizens was transferred, in the first instance, to the government of the United States; they became American citizens and owed obedience to the Constitution of the United States and to laws made in conformity with the powers it vested in Congress. [. . .]

How, then, with all these proofs that under all changes of our position we had, for designated purposes and with defined powers, created national governments, how is it that the most perfect of these several modes of union should now be considered as a mere league that may be dissolved at pleasure? It is from an abuse of terms. Compact is used as synonymous with league, although the true term is not employed, because it would at once show the

fallacy of the reasoning. It would not do to say that our Constitution was only a league, but it is labored to prove it a compact (which in one sense it is) and then to argue that as a league is a compact every compact between nations must of course be a league, and that from such an engagement every sovereign power has a right to recede. But it has been shown that in this sense the States are not sovereign, and that even if they were, and the national Constitution had been formed by compact, there would be no right in any one State to exonerate itself from its obligations.

This, then, is the position in which we stand. A small majority of the citizens of one State in the Union have elected delegates to a State convention; that convention has ordained that all the revenue laws of the United States must be repealed, or that they are no longer a member of the Union. The governor of that State has recommended to the legislature the raising of an army to carry the secession into effect, and that he may be empowered to give clearances to vessels in the name of the State. No act of violent opposition to the laws has yet been committed, but such a state of things is hourly apprehended. And it is the intent of this instrument to *proclaim*, not only that the duty imposed on me by the Constitution "to take care that the laws be faithfully executed" shall be performed to the extent of the powers already vested in me by law, or of such others as the wisdom of Congress shall devise and intrust to me for that purpose, but to warn the citizens of South Carolina who have been deluded into an opposition to the laws of the danger they will incur by obedience to the illegal and disorganizing ordinance of the convention; to exhort those who have refused to support it to persevere in their determination to uphold the Constitution and laws of their country; and to point out to all the perilous situation into which the good people of that state have been led, and that the course they am urged to pursue is one of ruin and disgrace to the very state whose rights they affect to support. [. . .]

If your leaders could succeed in establishing a separation, what would be your situation? Are you united at home? Are you free from the apprehension

of civil discord, with all its fearful consequences. Do our neighboring republics, every day suffering some new revolution or contending with some new insurrection, do they excite your envy? But the dictates of a high duty oblige me solemnly to announce that you can not succeed. The laws of the United States must be executed. I have no discretionary power on the subject; my duty is emphatically pronounced in the Constitution. Those who told you that you might peaceably prevent their execution deceived you; they could not have been deceived themselves. They know that a forcible opposition could alone prevent the execution of the laws, and they know that such opposition must be repelled. Their object is disunion. But be not deceived by names. Disunion by armed force is *treason*. Are you really ready to incur its guilt? If you are, on the heads of the instigators of the act be the dreadful consequences; on their heads be the dishonor, but on yours may fall the punishment. On your unhappy State will inevitably fall all the evils of the conflict you force upon the government of your country. It cannot accede to the mad project of disunion, of which you would be the first victims. Its First Magistrate cannot, if he would, avoid the performance of his duty. The consequence must be fearful for you, distressing to your fellow-citizens here and to the friends of good government throughout the world. Its enemies have beheld our prosperity with a vexation they could not conceal; to was a standing refutation of their slavish doctrines, and they will point to our discord with the triumph of malignant joy. It is yet in your power to disappoint them. [. . .]

Fellow-citizens of the United States, the threat of unhallowed disunion, the names of those once respected by whom it is uttered, the array of military force to support it, denote the approach of a crisis in our affairs on which the continuance of our unexampled prosperity, our political existence, and perhaps that of all free governments may depend. The conjuncture demanded a free, a full and explicit enunciation, not only of my intentions, but of my principles of action; and as the claim was asserted of a right by a state to annul the laws of the Union, and even to secede from it at pleasure, a frank exposi-

tion of my opinions in relation to the origin and form of our government and the construction I give to the instrument by which it was created seemed to be proper.

Having the fullest confidence in the justness of the legal and constitutional opinion of my duties which has been expressed, I rely with equal confidence on your undivided support in my determination to execute the laws, to preserve the Union by all constitutional means, to arrest, if possible, by moderate and firm measures the necessity of a recourse to force; and if it be the will of Heaven that the recurrence of its primeval curse on man for the shedding of a brother's blood should fall upon our land, that it be not called down by any offensive act on the part of the United States.

Fellow citizens, the momentous case is before you. On your undivided support of your Government depends the decision of the great question it involves—whether your sacred Union will be preserved and the blessing it secures to us as one people shall be perpetuated. No one can doubt that the unanimity with which that decision will be expressed will be such as to inspire new confidence in republican institutions, and that the prudence, the wisdom, and the courage which it will bring to their defense will transmit them unimpaired and invigorated to our children.

May the Great Ruler of Nations grant that the signal blessings with which He has favored ours may not, by the madness of party or personal ambition, be disregarded and lost; and may His wise providence bring those who have produced this crisis to see the folly before they feel the misery of civil strife, and inspire a returning veneration for that Union which, if we may dare to penetrate His designs, He has chosen as the only means of attaining the high destinies to which we may reasonably aspire.

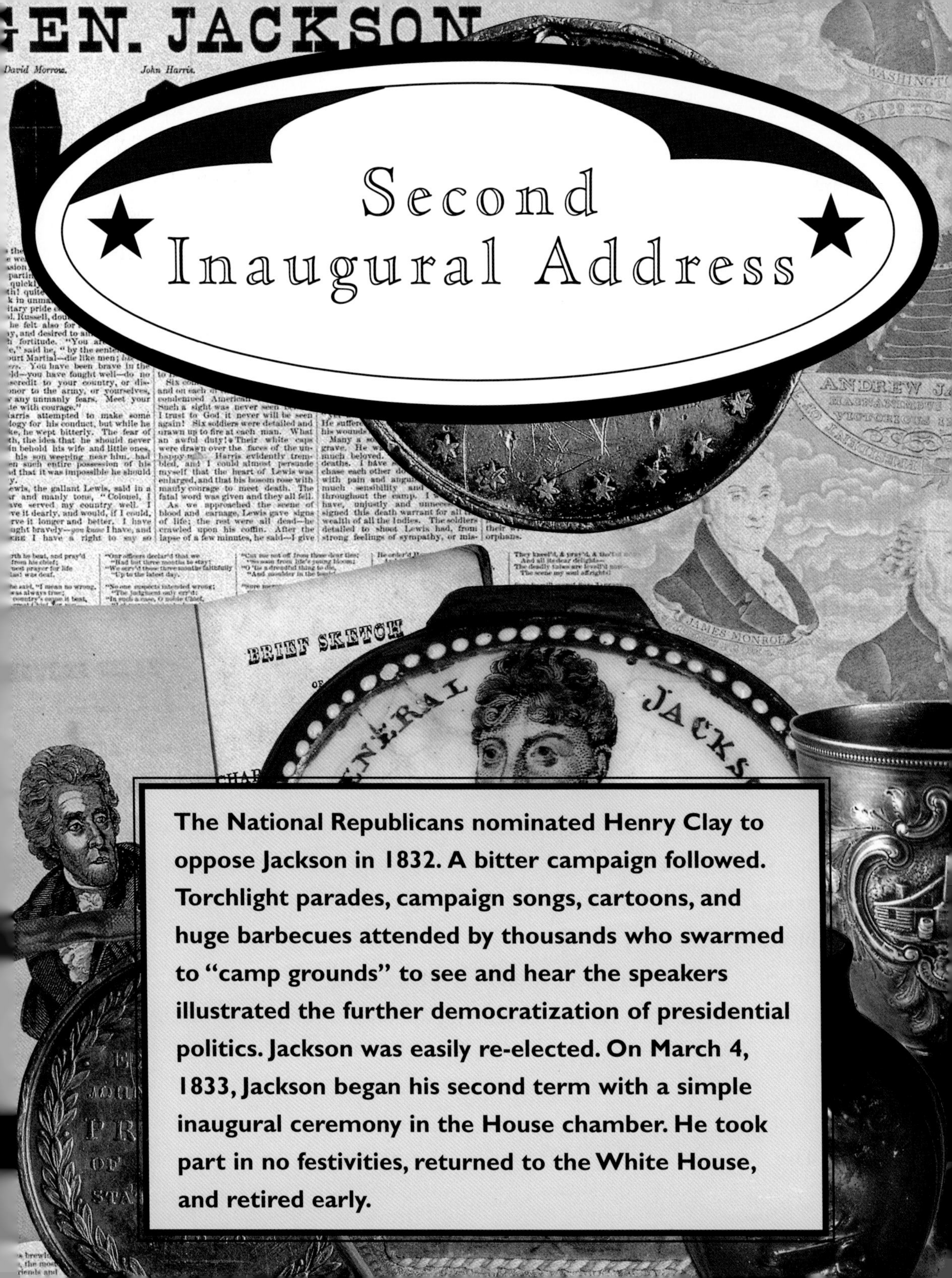

Second Inaugural Address

The National Republicans nominated Henry Clay to oppose Jackson in 1832. A bitter campaign followed. Torchlight parades, campaign songs, cartoons, and huge barbecues attended by thousands who swarmed to "camp grounds" to see and hear the speakers illustrated the further democratization of presidential politics. Jackson was easily re-elected. On March 4, 1833, Jackson began his second term with a simple inaugural ceremony in the House chamber. He took part in no festivities, returned to the White House, and retired early.

The will of the American people, expressed through their unsolicited suffrages, calls me before you to pass through the solemnities preparatory to taking upon myself the duties of President of the United States for another term. For their approbation of my public conduct through a period which has not been without its difficulties, and for this renewed expression of their confidence in my good intentions, I am at a loss for terms adequate to the expression of my gratitude. It shall be displayed to the extent of my humble abilities in continued efforts so to administer the Government as to preserve their liberty and promote their happiness.

So many events have occurred within the last four years which have necessarily called forth—sometimes under circumstances the most delicate and painful—my views of the principles and policy which ought to be pursued by the General Government that I need on this occasion but allude to a few leading considerations connected with some of them.

The foreign policy adopted by our Government soon after the formation of our present Constitution, and very generally pursued by successive Administrations, has been crowned with almost complete success, and has elevated our character among the nations of the earth. To do justice to all and to submit to wrong from none has been during my Administration its governing maxim, and so happy have been its results that we are not only at peace with all the world, but have few causes of controversy, and those of minor importance, remaining unadjusted.

In the domestic policy of this Government there are two objects which especially deserve the attention of the people and their representatives, and which have been and will continue to be the subjects of my increasing solicitude. They are the preservation of the rights of the several States and the integrity of the Union.

These great objects are necessarily connected, and can only be attained by an enlightened exercise of the powers of each within its appropriate sphere in conformity with the public will constitutionally expressed. To this end it becomes the duty of all to yield a ready and patriotic submission to the laws constitutionally enacted and thereby promote and strengthen a proper confidence in those institutions of the several States and of the United States which the people themselves have ordained for their own government.

My experience in public concerns and the observation of a life somewhat advanced confirm the opinions long since imbibed by me, that the destruction of our State governments or the annihilation of their control over the local concerns of the people would lead directly to revolution and anarchy, and finally to despotism and military domination. In proportion, therefore, as the General Government encroaches upon the rights of the States, in the same proportion does it impair its own power and detract from its ability to fulfill the purposes of its creation. Solemnly impressed with these considerations, my countrymen will ever find me ready to exercise my constitutional powers

Opposite: Jackson's controversial life inspired harsh negative campaigning. Several broadsides took issue with Jackson's "noble" military record. Many held "Old Hickory" accountable for excessive executions during the Creek War (1813–14). This is one of several broadsides featuring coffins.

With the victory of Andrew Jackson in 1828, something of a new democratic era began as the frontier creed, allied with the rise of the common man to political importance, won a national election. Jackson spoke about the important duties of the presidency, the need for a judicious tariff, lowering of the national debt, and the need for internal improvements, such as dams, canals, and roads, "so far as they can be promoted by the constitutional acts of the Federal Government." However, the major issue during his tenure in the White House was the Second Bank of the United States.

In 1832, the Jacksonians formally adopted the name Democrats. Two years later, the National Republicans, at Henry Clay's urging, changed their name to the Whig Party, symbolizing their opposition to "the reign of King Andrew." However, to Jackson's supporters, the great democratic society (for white people) of which Jackson had spoken almost reached fulfillment during his two administrations. It remained to be seen if Jackson's disciples could carry forward his political philosophy.

Some Account of some of the Bloody Deeds of GEN. JACKSON.

Jacob Webb. *David Morrow.* *John Harris.* *Henry Lewis.* *David Hunt.* *Edward Lindsey.*

A brief account of the Execution of the Six Militia Men.

As we may soon expect to have the *official* documents in relation to the SIX MILITIA MEN, arrested, tried, and put to death, under the orders of General Andrew Jackson, this may not be an improper time to give to the public some of the particulars of their execution, as we have them from "AN EYE WITNESS," who appeals to Col. Russell, for the truth of every word he relates.

Harris was a Baptist preacher, with a large family. He had hired as a substitute for three months. This was the case with most of them. They were ignorant men, but obstinate in what they believed right, and what they had been told by their officers was right. They were all sure they could not be kept beyond three months, and they gave up their muskets, and had provisions dealt out to them, from the public stores, before they left the camp. This confirmed their convictions that they were right, and doing what was lawful.

Col. Russell commanded at the execution. The Militia men were brought to the place in a large wagon. The military dispositions being made, Col. Russell rode up to the wagon and ordered the men to descend. Harris was the only one who betrayed feminine weakness. The awfulness of the occasion; his wife and nine children; the parting with his son; and the fear of a quickly approaching ignominious death! quite overcome him, and he sunk in unmanly grief. No feeling of military pride could brace him up.

Col. Russell, doubtless, felt as a man, but he felt also for the pride of the army, and desired to animate the men with fortitude. "You are about to "die," said he, "by the sentence of a "Court Martial—die like men; *like soldiers.* You have been brave in the "field—you have fought well—do no "discredit to your country, or dishonor to the army, or yourselves, "by any unmanly fears. Meet your "fate with courage."

Harris attempted to make some apology for his conduct, but while he spoke, he wept bitterly. The fear of death, the idea that he should never again behold his wife and little ones, and his son weeping near him, had taken such entire possession of his mind that it was impossible he should rally.

Lewis, the gallant Lewis, said in a clear and manly tone, "Colonel, I "have served my country well. I "love it dearly, and would, if I could, "serve it longer and better. I have "fought bravely—*you know* I have, and "HERE I have a right to say so "MYSELF. I would not wish to die in "this way"—here his voice faltered, "and he passed the back of his right "hand over his eyes—" I did not expect it. But, I am now as firm as I "have been in battle, and you shall see "that I will die as becomes a soldier; "you know I am a brave man." "Yes, Lewis," said the Colonel, "you "have always behaved like a brave "man." Other sentences were uttered, other declarations were made, and words of comfort spoken, but they were lost on me: my attention, says an Eye Witness, being chiefly directed to Lewis.

Six coffins were ranged as directed, and on each of them knelt one of our condemned American Militia Men. Such a sight was never seen before! I trust to God it never will be seen again! Six soldiers were detailed and drawn up to fire at each man. What an awful duty! Their white caps were drawn over the faces of the unhappy men. Harris evidently trembled, and I could almost persuade myself that the heart of Lewis was enlarged, and that his bosom rose with manly courage to meet death. The fatal word was given and they all fell.

As we approached the scene of blood and carnage, Lewis gave signs of life; the rest were all dead—he crawled upon his coffin. After the lapse of a few minutes, he said—I give his very words: "Colonel!"—the Colonel was close to him—"Colonel, I "am not killed, but I am sadly cut "and mangled." His body was now examined, and it was found that but four balls had wounded him. "Colonel, said he, "did I behave well?" "Yes, Lewis," said the Colonel in the kindest tone of voice, "like a man."—"Well, sir," said he, "have I not "atoned for this offence? *Shall I not "live?*" The Colonel was much agitated, and gave orders that the surgeon should, if possible, preserve his life. They did all that skill and humanity could do—it was all of no avail. Poor Lewis expressed a great desire to live—"not," said he at one time, "that I fear death, but I would repent "me of some sins, and I desire to live "yet a little longer in the world." He suffered inconceivable agony from his wounds and died on the fourth day.

Many a soldier has wept over his grave. He was a brave man and much beloved. He suffered twenty deaths. I have seen the big drops chase each other down his forehead with pain and anguish. There was much sensibility and sympathy throughout the camp. I would not have, unjustly and unnecessarily, signed this death warrant for all the wealth of all the Indies. The soldiers detailed to shoot Lewis had, from strong feelings of sympathy, or mistaken humanity, failed to shoot him—but four balls had entered his body.

"An Eye Witness" appeals to Col. Russell, who he thinks now lives in Alabama, for the perfect truth of this sketch. He does not fear but the Colonel will keenly recollect and faithfully depict the horrors of the day on which six Americans were shot to death under his command—but not by his orders.

The order bears date the very day after *General Jackson* returned in triumph to New Orleans, and the day before he joyfully went, under triumphal arches, to the temple of the living God; where, says the historian, "they crowned their adored General with laurels." The order for the execution of these six unhappy men bears date January 22, 1815. His crown of laurels had not yet withered when blood, the life's blood of his countrymen, of his fellow soldiers, flowed plentifully by his order. May that order and its consequences, sink deep into the hearts of the American people, and steel them against him who had no flesh in his obdurate heart; who did not feel for Man; in the midst of Joy and Revelry, almost in the more immediate presence of his Creator, who issued the fatal order to put his fellow creatures to death, and to make their wives and children, widows and orphans.

MOURNFUL TRAGEDY;

Or, the death of Jacob Webb, David Morrow, John Harris, Henry Lewis, David Hunt and Edward Lindsey—six militia men—who were condemned to die, the sentence approved by Major General JACKSON, and by his order the whole six shot.

O! did you hear that plaintive cry
Borne on the southern breeze?
Saw you John Harris earnest pray
For mercy, on his knees?

Low to the earth he bent, and pray'd
For pardon from his chief;
But to his earnest prayer for life
JACKSON, alas! was deaf.

"Spare me," he said, "I mean no wrong,
"My heart was always true;
"First for my country's cause it beat,
"And next, great Chief, for you.

"We thought our time of service out—
"Thought it our right to go;
"We meant to violate no law,
"Nor wish'd to shun the foe.

"Our officers declar'd that we
"Had but three months to stay;
"We serv'd those three months faithfully
"Up to the latest day.

"No one suspects intended wrong;
"The judgment only err'd;
"In such a case, O noble Chief,
"Let mercy's voice be heard.

"At home an aged mother waits
"To clasp her only son;
"A wife, and little children—this arm
"Alone depend upon.

"Cut me not off from those dear ties;
"Sever'd from life's young bloom;
"O 'tis a dreadful thing to die,
"And moulder in the tomb!

"Sure mercy is a noble gem
"On every Chieftain's brow;
"More sparkling than a diadem—
"O exercise it now."—

'Twas all in vain, John Harris' pray'r,
Tho' past the soul's belief!
Hard as the flint was Jackson's heart;
He would not grant relief.

He order'd Harris out to die,
And five poor fellows more!
Young, gallant men, in prime of life,
To welter in their gore!!

Methinks I hear the muffled drum,
And see the column move;
Lo here they come—how sad their looks!
Farewell to life and love!

See six black coffins rang'd along—
Six graves before them made;
Webb, Lindsey, Harris, Lewis, Hunt,
And Morrow kneel'd and pray'd.

They kneel'd, & pray'd, & thought of home,
And all its dear delights—
The deadly tubes are level'd now—
The scene my soul affrights!

Sure he will spare! Sure JACKSON yet
Will all reprieve but one—
O hark! those shrieks! that cry of death!
The dreadful deed is done!

All six militia men were shot?
And O! it seems to me
A dreadful deed—a bloody act
Of needless cruelty.

The reader is reminded that it was on the 21st day of January, 1815, that General Jackson returned to the city of New Orleans from the battle ground. The British had abandoned the enterprise and retired. The General was received with the strongest demonstrations of joy and attachment. It was on that very day, January 21, that he issued the order for the execution of the six militia-men. The 23d was appointed a day of general thanksgiving, when the General was provided with a wreath of laurel by the hands of the Bishop. On the 28th of the same month an order was issued for the execution of twelve soldiers, condemned by a Court Martial at Nashville. All to be executed within four days after the promulgation of the order!!

"[Extract from the General Order, dated 'Adjutant General's Office, New Orleans, January 28th, 1815, Head Quarters, 7th Military District,' on the proceedings of the General Court Martial, held at Nashville on the 19th of October, 1814, and continued by adjournment till the 25th of November, 1814.]"

"Was also tried the following-named men, soldiers of the army of the United States, severally charged with 'desertion,' viz.: Richard Wall, of 3d Rifle Regiment; Jacob Perregrin, of said Regiment; both of Capt. Willey Martin's company; John Jones, of the 24th Regiment of Infantry; William Myers, of Capt. Humphrey's company of Artillery; Jacob King, of Capt. Reed's company, said corps; Benjamin Harris, of the 44th Infantry; John Young, of the 39th Infantry; Nathaniel Chester, of the corps of Artillery; Drury Puckett, of the 24th Infantry; Wyat Grantt, of the 39th Infantry; Joseph Muckelroy, of the 24th Infantry; and James McBride, 2d Rifle Regiment; to which charge they severally pleaded Not Guilty, except Jacob King, who pleaded Guilty. The Court, after the examination of testimony on each of the cases, and deliberation had thereon, pronounce on each and every one of them 'Death by shooting.' The Major General approves the sentence passed on the above named soldiers of the Army of the United States, and orders the same to be carried into full effect in four days after the promulgation of this order, at the post where they may be, under the direction of the senior officer present."

Another was to have been executed at the same time. He was a young man, who had deserted one month before his time had expired. General Jackson doomed him to die with the others. He was saved by a writ of habeas corpus from Judge M'Nairy, who fell under Jackson's displeasure for snatching this one victim from his blood stained hands. If Jackson's army had been at hand, no doubt M'Nairy would have shared the fate of Judge Hall and Judge Fromentin. Capital punishments in an army, are designed for example as well as for penalty; but in this case it was a transaction of horror to peaceful citizens: no army was there to witness the bloody tragedy. He has ever been a man of "blood and carnage."

There can be no doubt that every one of these men were executed. There was no power to save them after the promulgation of this order. Thus we see that Gen. Jackson, within the space of one week, in the midst of exultations and rejoicings, ordered eighteen of his fellow men to be put to death!!! Is there any instance on record, in any history of modern warfare, that equals this for barbarity? The time, the circumstances, the numbers. And can it be that this barbarian shall be elevated to the chief magistracy of a free, a generous, and a merciful nation?

Do not be startled, gentle reader, at the picture before you. It is all true and every body ought to know it. Gen. Jackson having made an assault upon Samuel Jackson, in the streets of Nashville, and the latter not being disposed to stand still and be beaten, stooped down for a stone to defend himself—While in the act of doing so, Gen. Jackson drew the sword from his cane and run it thro' Sam'l Jackson's body, the sword entering his back and coming out of his breast. For this offence an Indictment was found against Gen. Jackson, by a grand jury, upon which he was subsequently arraigned and tried. But finding means to persuade the petit jury that he committed the act in self defence, he was acquitted. Gentle reader, it is for you to say, whether this man, who carries a sword cane, and is willing to run it thro' the body of any one who may presume to stand in his way, is a fit person to be our President.

Poor JOHN WOODS; he was a generous hearted, noble fellow as ever lived, who had volunteered in the service of his country. He was on guard one day at Fort Strother—the officer of the guard had permitted him to go to his tent, and snatch a hasty breakfast; whilst disposing of his scanty meal, seated on the ground beside his skillet, an upstart little officer, who was not Wood's equal at home, ordered him to pick up and carry off some bones that lay scattered about the place—Woods refused, and the little officer attempted to compel him. At this instant, Gen. Jackson, having heard the dispute, came out of his tent, and without knowing any thing of the merits of the case, repeatedly vociferated—"*Shoot the damn'd rascal!—Shoot the damn'd rascal.*" For this offence, the unfortunate, the gallant Woods, was tried, condemned and shot. Before his trial, Gen. Jackson used this language to the court-martial. "*By the immortal God! if you find him guilty I will not pardon him!*" And he kept his promise; though he did offer a pardon provided he would enlist in the regular service—Thus perished as noble a fellow as ever lived, for as trifling an offence as ever took the life of man!!!

On the 27th day of March, 1814, General Jackson had found at an Indian village, at the bend of the Tallapoosa, about 4000 Indians, with their *squaws and children*, "running about among their huts." The following is an account of the sanguinary massacre which took place—it is Gen. Jackson's own, and therefore must be received as sufficient evidence against himself. He says:—"DETERMINING TO EXTERMINATE them, I detached Gen. Coffee with the mounted men and nearly the whole of the Indian force, early on the morning of yesterday, to cross the river about two miles below the encampment, that none of them should escape by attempting to cross the river." The result he then details:—"*Five hundred and fifty-seven were left dead on the Peninsula, and a great number of them were killed by the horsemen attempting to cross the river.* IT IS BELIEVED THAT NO MORE THAN TEN ESCAPED. WE CONTINUED TO DESTROY *many of them who had concealed themselves under the banks of the river, until we were prevented by the night.* THIS MORNING WE KILLED 16 WHICH HAD BEEN CONCEALED."

We ask you to pause and reflect that the above tragic narration of cold blooded and merciless cruelty, is taken from an official communication, made by General Andrew Jackson.

The General, after sleeping (with what composure, we cannot say) through the night ensuing the tragedy we speak of, awoke in the morning surrounded by the corpses of "five hundred and seventy" fellow creatures, to cause, by way of worthy afterpiece, sixteen others to be dragged from their concealments, and put to death in cold blood. We cannot boast of more than common sensibility, but we must think that to witness such an act, would make ours a little cold also. What are the general's words?—these: "this morning we killed sixteen which had been concealed!"—and the man who acts and speaks thus; who has half as much blood upon his conscience, as he has upon his hands—he, forsooth, is to be called the peer and like of Washington, the happy warrior,——————" he Whom every man at arms would wish to be."

But it is time to have done with the unpleasant subject. We will observe in addition to the details already given, that the village was burnt, and several women and children killed. In conclusion, we ask our fellow citizens, whether Gen. Jackson though he has contributed largely to the military reputation of our country, has not done enough to disqualify him, in the eyes of the people as virtuous as they are free, for the office he seeks at their hands.

Gen. Jackson, detailing his progress among the Indians, in the course of which, men, WOMEN and CHILDREN, were indiscriminately "exterminated," their towns burnt, and their country laid waste, with the utmost complacency and *sang froid*, says, in his letter dated, "Camp before St. Marks, April 9, 1818—"Captain McEver having hoisted English colours on board of his boats, Francis the *Prophet*, Hoemoehemotcho, and *two others*, were *decoyed* on board *These have been hung to-day!*" Reader, mark the perfect indifference with which Gen. Jackson shoots, hangs or stabs his fellow beings, with or without trial, and the more than callous, aye, even exulting composure, with which he details his horrid and bloody deeds! If the Indians, according to the customs of their nation, put to death a prisoner, all the feelings of our nature rise into indignation against them. With what feelings then should we contemplate the *decoying* & the cold-blooded murder of prisoners, by a civilized man, in the face of the laws and customs of his country.

FRANKLIN, Tenn. September 10, 1818.

A difference which had been for some months brewing between Gen. Jackson and myself, produced on Saturday, 4th inst. in the town of Nashville, the most outrageous affray ever witnessed in a civilized country. In communicating the affair to my friends and fellow citizens, I limit myself to the statement of a few leading facts, the truth of which I am ready to establish by judicial proofs.

1. That myself and my brother, Jesse Benton, arriving in Nashville on the morning of the affray, and knowing of Gen. Jackson's threats, went and took lodgings in a different house from the one in which he staid, on purpose to avoid him.

2. That the Gen. and some of his friends came to the house where we had put up and commenced the attack by leveling a pistol at me, when I had no weapon drawn, and advancing upon me at a quick pace without giving me time to draw one.

3. That seeing this, my brother fired upon Gen. Jackson, when he had got within eight or ten feet of me.

4. That four other pistols were fired in quick succession; one by Gen. Jackson at me; two by me at the Gen.; and one by Col. Coffee at me. In the course of this firing, Gen. Jackson was brought to the ground; but received no hurt.

5. That daggers were then drawn. Col. Coffee and Mr. Alexander Donaldson made at me, and gave me five slight wounds. Capt. Hammond and Mr. Stokeley Hays engaged my brother, who, being still weak from the effects of a severe wound he had lately received in a duel, was not able to resist two men. They got him down; and while Capt. Hammond beat him on the head to make him lie still, Mr. Hays attempted to stab him, and wounded him in both arms, as he lay on his back parrying the thrusts with his naked hands. From this situation a generous hearted citizen of Nashville, Mr. Summer, relieved him. Before he came to the ground, my brother clapped a pistol to the breast of Mr. Hays to blow him through, but it missed fire.

6. My own and my brother's pistols carried two balls each; for it was our intention, if driven to arms, to have no child's play. The pistols fired at me were so near that the blaze of the muzzle of one of them burnt the sleeve of my coat, and the other, aimed at my head at a little more than arm's length from it.

7. Capt. Carroll was to have taken part in the affray, but was absent by the permission of Gen. Jackson, as he has proved by the General's certificate; a certificate which reflects I know not whether less honour upon the General or upon the Captain.

8. That this attack was made upon me in the house where the Judge of the District, Mr. Searcy, had his lodgings! Nor has the civil authority yet taken cognizance of this horrible outrage.

These facts are sufficient to fix the public opinion. For my own part, I think it scandalous that such things should take place at any time; but particularly so at the present moment, when the public service requires the aid of all its citizens. As for the *name of courage*, God forbid that I should ever attempt to gain it by becoming a bully. Those who know me, know full well that I would give a thousand times more for the reputation of Croghan in defending his post, than I would for the reputation of all the duelists and gladiators that ever appeared upon the face of the earth.

THOMAS HART BENTON, *Lieut. Col. Thirty-Ninth Infantry*
And now a member of the Senate of the United States.

in arresting measures which may directly or indirectly encroach upon the rights of the States or tend to consolidate all political power in the General Government. But of equal and, indeed of incalculable, importance is the union of these States, and the sacred duty of all to contribute to its preservation by a liberal support of the General Government in the exercise of its just powers. You have been wisely admonished to "accustom yourselves to think and speak of the Union as of the palladium of your political safety and prosperity, watching for its preservation with jealous anxiety, discountenancing whatever may suggest even a suspicion that it can in any event be abandoned, and indignantly frowning upon the first dawning of any attempt to alienate any portion of our country from the rest or to enfeeble the sacred ties which now link together the various parts." Without union our independence and liberty would never have been achieved; without union they never can be maintained. Divided into twenty-four, or even a smaller number, of separate communities, we shall see our internal trade burdened with numberless restraints and exactions; communication between distant points and sections obstructed or cut off; our sons made soldiers to deluge with blood the fields they now till in peace; the mass of our people borne down and impoverished by taxes to support armies and navies, and military leaders at the head of their victorious legions becoming our lawgivers and judges. The loss of liberty, of all good government, of peace, plenty, and happiness, must inevitably follow a dissolution of the Union. In supporting it, therefore, we support all that is dear to the freeman and the philanthropist.

The time at which I stand before you is full of interest. The eyes of all nations are fixed on our Republic. The event of the existing crisis will be decisive in the opinion of mankind of the practicability of our federal system of government. Great is the stake placed in our hands; great is the responsibility which must rest upon the people of the United States. Let us realize the importance of the attitude in which we stand before the world. Let us exercise forbearance and firmness. Let us extricate our country from the dangers

which surround it and learn wisdom from the lessons they inculcate.

Deeply impressed with the truth of these observations, and under the obligation of that solemn oath which I am about to take, I shall continue to exert all my faculties to maintain the just powers of the Constitution and to transmit unimpaired to posterity the blessings of our Federal Union. At the same time, it will be my aim to inculcate by my official acts the necessity of exercising by the General Government those powers only that are clearly delegated; to encourage simplicity and economy in the expenditures of the Government; to raise no more money from the people than may be requisite for these objects, and in a manner that will best promote the interests of all classes of the community and of all portions of the Union. Constantly bearing in mind that in entering into society "individuals must give up a share of liberty to preserve the rest," it will be my desire so to discharge my duties as to foster with our brethren in all parts of the country a spirit of liberal concession and compromise, and, by reconciling our fellow-citizens to those partial sacrifices which they must unavoidably make for the preservation of a greater good, to recommend our invaluable Government and Union to the confidence and affections of the American people.

Finally, it is my most fervent prayer to that Almighty Being before whom I now stand, and who has kept us in His hands from the infancy of our Republic to the present day, that He will so overrule all my intentions and actions and inspire the hearts of my fellow-citizens that we may be preserved from dangers of all kinds and continue forever a united and happy people.

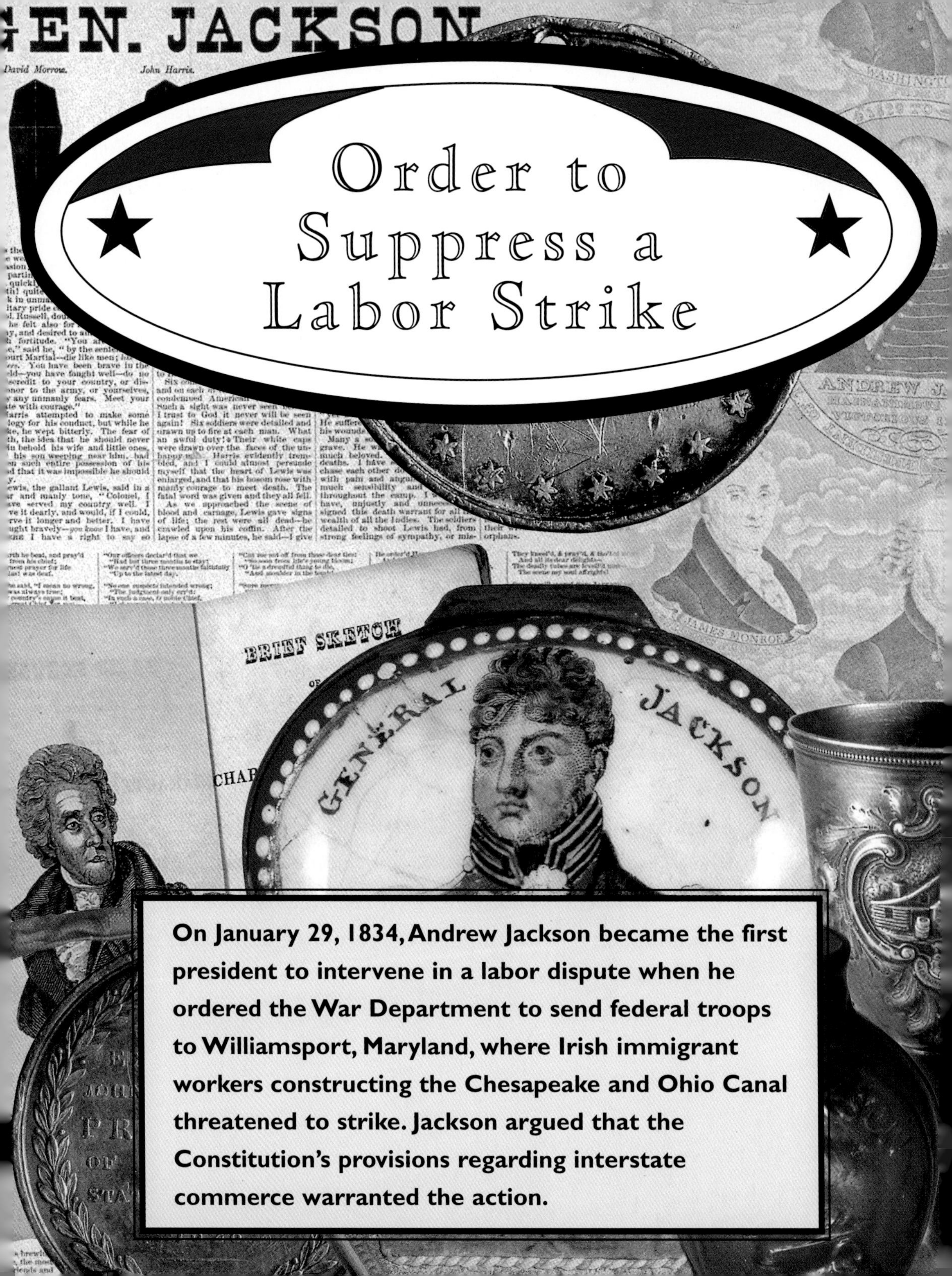

Order to Suppress a Labor Strike

On January 29, 1834, Andrew Jackson became the first president to intervene in a labor dispute when he ordered the War Department to send federal troops to Williamsport, Maryland, where Irish immigrant workers constructing the Chesapeake and Ohio Canal threatened to strike. Jackson argued that the Constitution's provisions regarding interstate commerce warranted the action.

The Secretary of War will forthwith order such military as will be able to aid the civil authority of Maryland to put down the riotous assembly named within [on the Chesapeake and Ohio Canal]—at least two companies of regulars with as much expedition as possible.

Andrew Jackson's Farewell Speech

President Andrew Jackson's administration ranks as one of the most important in American history. He was not a theorist. He met issues as they arose. Jackson lived in a time of heroes—and he must be considered one of America's greatest heroes with all of the glamour that goes with such a personality. On the morning he left office (March 4, 1837), Jackson published his Farewell Address. He appealed for loyalty to the Union. On this issue he never equivocated or compromised.

Being about to retire finally from public life, I beg leave to offer you my grateful thanks for the many proofs of kindness and confidence which I have received at your hands. It has been my fortune, in the discharge of public duties, civil and military, frequently to have found myself in difficult and trying situations where prompt decision and energetic action were necessary and where the interest of the country required that high responsibilities should be fearlessly encountered; and it is with the deepest emotions of gratitude that I acknowledge the continued and unbroken confidence with which you have sustained me in every trial. My public life has been a long one, and I cannot hope that it has, at all times, been free from errors. But I have the consolation of knowing that, if mistakes have been committed, they have not seriously injured the country I so anxiously endeavored to serve; and, at the moment when I surrender my last public trust, I leave this great people prosperous and happy; in the full enjoyment of liberty and peace; and honored and respected by every nation of the world.

If my humble efforts have, in any degree, contributed to preserve to you these blessings, I have been more than rewarded by the honors you have heaped upon me; and, above all, by the generous confidence with which you have supported me in every peril, and with which you have continued to animate and cheer my path to the closing hour of my political life. The time has now come when advanced age and a broken frame warn me to retire from public concerns; but the recollection of the many favors you have bestowed upon me is engraven upon my heart, and I have felt that I could not part from your service without making this public acknowledgment of the gratitude I owe you. And if I use the occasion to offer to you the counsels of age and experience, you will, I trust, receive them with the same indulgent kindness which you have so often extended to me; and will, at least, see in them an earnest desire to perpetuate, in this favored land, the blessings of liberty and equal laws.

THE STATE OF THE NATION

We have now lived almost fifty years under the Constitution framed by the sages and patriots of the Revolution. The conflicts in which the nations of Europe were engaged during a great part of this period; the spirit in which they waged war against each other; and our intimate commercial connections with every part of the civilized world, rendered it a time of much difficulty for the Government of the United States. We have had our seasons of peace and of war, with all the evils which precede or follow a state of hostility with powerful nations. We encountered these trials with our Constitution yet in its infancy, and under the disadvantages which a new and untried Government must always feel when it is called upon to put forth its whole strength, without the lights of experience to guide it or the weight of precedents to justify its measures. But we have passed triumphantly through all these difficulties. Our Constitution is no longer a doubtful experiment; and, at the end of nearly half a century, we find that it has preserved unimpaired the liberties of the people, secured the rights of property, and that our country has improved and is flourishing beyond any former example in the history of nations.

In our domestic concerns there is everything to encourage us; and if you are true to yourselves, nothing can impede your march to the highest point of national prosperity. The States which had so long been retarded in their improvement by the Indian tribes residing in the midst of them are at length relieved from the evil; and this unhappy race—the original dwellers in our land—are now placed in a situation where we may well hope that they will share in the blessings of civilization and be saved from that degradation and destruction to which they were rapidly hastening while they remained in the States; and while the safety and comfort of our own citizens have been greatly promoted by their removal, the philanthropist will rejoice that the remnant of that ill-fated race has been at length placed beyond the reach of

injury or oppression, and that the paternal care of the General Government will hereafter watch over them and protect them.

If we turn to our relations with foreign powers, we find our condition equally gratifying. Actuated by the sincere desire to do justice to every nation and to preserve the blessings of peace, our intercourse with them has been conducted on the part of this Government in the spirit of frankness, and I take pleasure in saying that it has generally been met in a corresponding temper. Difficulties of old standing have been surmounted by friendly discussion and the mutual desire to be just; and the claims of our citizens, which had been long withheld, have at length been acknowledged and adjusted, and satisfactory arrangements made for their final payment; and with a limited and, I trust, a temporary exception, our relations with every foreign power are now of the most friendly character, our commerce continually expanding, and our flag respected in every quarter of the world.

THE NEED FOR UNITY IN THE UNION

These cheering and grateful prospects and these multiplied favors we owe, under Providence, to the adoption of the Federal Constitution. It is no longer a question whether this great country can remain happily united and flourish under our present form of government.Experience, the unerring test of all human undertakings, has shown the wisdom and foresight of those who formed it; and has proved that in the union of these States there is a sure foundation for the brightest hopes of freedom and for the happiness of the people. At every hazard and by every sacrifice, this Union must be preserved.

The necessity of watching with jealous anxiety for the preservation of the Union was earnestly pressed upon his fellow citizens by the Father of his country in his farewell address. He has there told us that "while experience shall not have demonstrated its impracticability, there will always be reason to distrust the patriotism of those who, in any quarter, may endeavor to weaken its bonds"; and he has cautioned us, in the strongest terms, against the formation of parties on geographical discriminations, as one of the means which might disturb our union, and to which designing men would be likely to the resort.

The lessons contained in this invaluable legacy of Washington to his countrymen should be cherished in the heart of every citizen to the latest generation; and, perhaps, at no period of time could they be more usefully remembered than at the present moment. For when we look upon the scenes that are passing around us, and dwell upon the pages of his parting address, his paternal counsels would seem to be not merely the offspring of wisdom and foresight, but the voice of prophecy foretelling events and warning us of the evil to come. Forty years have passed since this imperishable document was given to his countrymen. The Federal Constitution was then regarded by him as an experiment, and he so speaks of it in his address; but an experiment upon the success of which the best hopes of his country depended, and we all know that he was prepared to lay down his life, if necessary, to secure to it a full and a fair trial. The trial has been made. It has succeeded beyond the proudest hopes of those who framed it. Every quarter of this widely extended nation has felt its blessings and shared in the general prosperity produced by its adoption. But amid this general prosperity and splendid success, the dangers of which he warned us are becoming every day more evident and the signs of evil are sufficiently apparent to awaken the deepest anxiety in the bosom of the patriot. We behold systematic efforts publicly made to sow the seeds of discord between different parts of the United States and to place party divisions directly upon geographical distinctions; to excite the south against the north and the north against the south; and to force into the controversy the most delicate and exciting topics, topics upon which it is impossible that a large portion of the Union can ever speak without strong emotion. Appeals, too, are constantly made to sectional interests in order to influence the election of the Chief Magistrate, as if it were desired that he should favor a particular quarter of the country instead of fulfilling the duties

Pewter-rimmed medallions with lithographed portraits under glass of the 1828 presidential opponents, Jackson and Adams.

The burning issue of slavery intensified during Jackson's administration. With the fatalism of a Greek tragedy, the nation appeared to be rushing toward destruction.

Jackson warned of the dangers emanating from sectional disagreements over slavery that based party differences only on geographic distinctions, but he could not bring himself to oppose slavery. John Quincy Adams opposed the expansion of slavery and at heart was an abolitionist, although he never became one in the political sense of the word.

of his station with impartial justice to all; and the possible dissolution of the Union has at length become an ordinary and familiar subject of discussion. Has the warning voice of Washington been forgotten? Or have designs already been formed to sever the Union? Let it not be supposed that I impute to all of those who have taken an active part in these unwise and unprofitable discussions a want of patriotism or of public virtue. The honorable feeling of State pride and local attachments find a place in the bosoms of the most enlightened and pure. But while such men are conscious of their own integrity and honesty of purpose, they ought never to forget that the citizens of other States are their political brethren; and that, however mistaken they may be in their views, the great body of them are equally honest and upright with themselves. Mutual suspicions and reproaches may in time create mutual hostility, and artful and designing men will always be found, who are ready to to foment these fatal divisions and to inflame the natural jealousies of different sections of the country. The history of the world is full of such examples and especially the history of republics.

What have you to gain by division and dissension? Delude not yourselves with the belief that a breach once made may be afterwards repaired. If the Union is once severed, the line of separation will grow wider and wider, and the controversies which are now debated and settled in the halls of legislation will then be tried in fields of battle and determined by the sword. Neither should you deceive yourselves with the hope that the first line of separation would be the permanent one, and that nothing but harmony and concord would be found in the new associations formed upon the dissolution of this Union. Local interests would still be found there, and unchastened ambition. And if the recollection of common dangers in which the people of these United States stood side by side against the common foe; the memory of victories won by their united valor; the prosperity and happiness they have enjoyed under the present Constitution; the proud name they bear as citizens of this great republic; if all these recollections and proofs of common interest are not strong enough to bind us together as one people, what tie will hold united the new divisions of empire, when these bonds have been broken and this Union dissevered? The first line of separation would not last for a single generation; new fragments would be torn off; new leaders would spring up; and this great and glorious republic would soon be broken into a multitude of petty states, without commerce, without credit; jealous of one another; armed for mutual aggression; loaded with taxes to pay armies and leaders; seeking aid against each other from foreign powers; insulted and trampled upon by the nations of

Europe, until, harassed with conflicts and humbled and debased in spirit, they would be ready to submit to the absolute dominion of any military adventurer and to surrender their liberty for the sake of repose. It is impossible to look on the consequences that would inevitably follow the destruction of this Government and not feel indignant when we hear cold calculations about the value of the Union and have so constantly before us a line of conduct so well calculated to weaken its ties.

There is too much at stake to allow pride or passion to influence unless he clearly saw that the time had come when a freeman should prefer death to submission; for if such a struggle is once begun and the citizens of any State or States can deliberately intend to do wrong. They may, under the influence of temporary excitement or misguided opinions, commit mistakes; they may be misled for a time by the suggestions of self-interest; but in a community so enlightened and patriotic as the people of the United States, argument will soon make them sensible of their errors; and, when convinced, they will be ready to repair them. If they have no higher or better motives to govern them, they will at least perceive that their own interest requires them to be just to others as they hope to receive justice at their hands.

NULLIFICATION AND STATES' RIGHTS

But in order to maintain the Union unimpaired, it is absolutely necessary that the laws passed by the constituted authorities should be faithfully executed in every part of the country, and that every good citizen should, at all times, stand ready to put down, with the combined force of the nation, every attempt at unlawful resistance, under whatever pretext it may be made or whatever shape it may assume. Unconstitutional or oppressive laws may no doubt be passed by Congress, either from erroneous views or the want of due consideration; if they are within the reach of judicial authority, the remedy is easy and peaceful; and if, from the character of the law, it is an abuse of power not within the control of the judiciary, then free discussion and calm appeals to reason and to the justice of the people will not fail to redress the wrong. But until the law shall be declared void by the courts or repealed by Congress, no individual or combination of individuals can be justified in forcibly resisting its execution. It is impossible that any Government can continue to exist upon any other principles. It would cease to be a Government and be unworthy of the name if it had not the power to enforce the execution of its own laws within its own sphere of action.

It is true that cases may be imagined disclosing such a settled purpose of usurpation and oppression on the part of the Government as would justify an appeal to arms. These, however, are extreme cases, which we have no reason to apprehend in a Government where the power is in the hands of a patriotic people; and no citizen who loves his country would in any case whatever resort to forcible resistance, unless he clearly saw that the time had come when a freeman should prefer death to submission; for if such a struggle is once begun and the citizens of one section of the country arrayed in arms against those of another in doubtful conflict, let the battle result as it may, there will be an end of the Union and, with it, an end to the hopes of freedom. The victory of the injured would not secure to them the blessings of liberty; it would avenge their wrongs, but they would themselves share in the common ruin. [. . .]

LIMITS OF FEDERAL POWERS

It is well known that there have always been those amongst us who wish to enlarge the powers of the General Government; and experience would seem to indicate that there is a tendency on the part of this Government to overstep the boundaries marked out for it by the Constitution. Its legitimate authority is abundantly sufficient for all the purposes for which it was created; and its powers being expressly enumerated, there can be no justification for claiming anything beyond them. Every attempt to exercise power beyond these limits should be promptly and firmly opposed. For one evil example will lead to other measures still more mischievous; and if the principle of constructive powers, or supposed advantages, or temporary circumstances, shall ever be permitted to justify the assumption of a power not given by the Constitution, the General Government will before long absorb all the powers of legislation, and you will have, in effect, but one consolidated Government. From the extent of our country, its diversified interests, different pursuits, and different habits, it is too obvious for argument that a single consolidated Government would be wholly inadequate to watch over and protect its interests; and every friend of our free institutions should be always prepared to maintain unimpaired and in full vigor the rights and sovereignty of the States and to confine the action of the General Government strictly to the sphere of its appropriate duties.

There is, perhaps, no one of the powers conferred on the Federal Government so liable to abuse as the taxing power. The most productive and convenient sources of revenue were necessarily given to it, that it might be able to perform the important duties imposed upon it; and the taxes which it lays upon commerce being concealed from the real payer in the price of the article, they do not so readily attract the attention of the people as smaller sums demanded from them directly by the tax gatherer. But the tax imposed on goods enhances by so much the price of the commodity to the consumer, and, as many of these duties are imposed on articles of necessity which are daily used by the great body of the people, the money raised by these imposts is drawn from their pockets. Congress has no right, under the Constitution, to take money from the people unless it is required to execute some one of the specific powers intrusted to the Government; and if they raise more than is necessary for such purposes, it is an abuse of the power of taxation and unjust and oppressive. It may, indeed, happen that the revenue will sometimes exceed the amount anticipated when the taxes were laid. When, however, this is ascertained, it is easy to reduce them; and, in such a case, it is unquestionably the duty of the Government to reduce them, for no circumstances can justify it in assuming a power not given to it by the Constitution nor in taking away the money of the people when it is not needed for the legitimate wants of the Government.

CURRENCY AND BANKING POLICY

In reviewing the conflicts which have taken place between different interests in the United States and the policy pursued since the adoption of our present form of government, we find nothing that has produced such deep-seated evil as the course of legislation in relation to the currency. The Constitution of the United States unquestionably intended to secure to the people a circulating medium of gold and silver. But the establishment of a national bank by Congress with the privilege of issuing paper money receivable in the payment of the public dues, and the unfortunate course of legislation in the several States upon the same subject, drove from general circulation the constitutional currency and substituted one of paper in its place.

It was not easy for men engaged in the ordinary pursuits of business, whose attention had not been particularly drawn to the subject, to foresee all the consequences of a currency exclusively of paper; and we ought not, on that account, to be surprised at the facility with which laws were obtained to carry into effect the paper system. Honest and even enlightened men are sometimes misled by the specious and plausible statements of the designing. But experience has now proved the mischiefs and dangers of a paper currency, and it rests with you to determine whether the proper remedy shall be applied.

The paper system being founded on public confidence and having of itself no intrinsic value, it is liable to great and sudden fluctuations; thereby rendering property insecure and the wages of labor unsteady and uncertain. The corporations which create the paper money can not be relied upon to keep the circulating medium uniform in amount. In times of prosperity when confidence is high, they are tempted by the prospect of gain, or by the influence of those who hope to profit by it to extend their issues of paper beyond the bounds of discretion and the reasonable demands of business. And when these issues have been pushed on from day to day until public confidence is at

length shaken, then a reaction takes place, and they immediately withdraw the credits they have given; suddenly curtail their issues; and produce an unexpected and ruinous contraction of the circulating medium which is felt by the whole community. The banks by this means save themselves, and the mischievous consequences of their imprudence or cupidity are visited upon the public. Nor does the evil stop here. These ebbs and flows in the currency and these indiscreet extensions of credit naturally engender a spirit of speculation injurious to the habits and character of the people. We have already seen its effects in the wild spirit of speculation in the public lands and various kinds of stock which, within the last year or two, seized upon such a multitude of our citizens and threatened to pervade all classes of society and to withdraw their attention from the sober pursuits of honest industry. It is not by encouraging this spirit that we shall best preserve public virtue and promote the true interests of our country. But if your currency continues as exclusively paper as it now is, it will foster this eager desire to amass wealth without labor; it will multiply the number of dependents on bank accommodations and bank favors; the temptation to obtain money at any sacrifice

The earliest campaign music dates from 1800. With the 1828 campaign, elaborate candidate portraits decorated sheet music.

will become stronger and stronger, and inevitably lead to corruption which will find its way into your public councils and destroy, at no distant day, the purity of your Government. Some of the evils which arise from this system of paper press with peculiar hardship upon the class of society least able to bear it. A portion of this currency frequently becomes depreciated or worthless, and all of it is easily counterfeited in such a manner as to require peculiar skill and much experience to distinguish the counterfeit from the genuine note. These frauds are most generally perpetrated in the smaller notes, which are used in the daily transactions of ordinary business; and the losses occasioned by them are commonly thrown upon the laboring classes of society whose situation and pursuits put it out of their power to guard themselves from these impositions and whose daily wages are necessary for their subsistence. It is the duty of every Government so to regulate its currency as to protect this numerous class as far as practicable from the impositions of avarice and fraud. It is more especially the duty of the United States where the Government is emphatically the Government of the people, and where this respectable portion of our citizens are so proudly distinguished from the laboring classes of all other nations by their independent spirit, their love of liberty, their intelligence, and their high tone of moral character. Their industry in peace is the source of our wealth; and their bravery in war has covered us with glory; and the Government of the United States will but ill discharge its duties if it leaves them a prey to such dishonest impositions. Yet it is evident that their interests cannot be effectually protected unless silver and gold are restored to circulation.

THOUGHTS ON FOREIGN POLICY AND NATIONAL DEFENSE

While I am thus endeavoring to press upon your attention the principles which I deem of vital importance in the domestic concerns of the country, I ought not to pass over, without notice, the important considerations which should govern your policy toward foreign powers. It is, unquestionably, our true interest to cultivate the most friendly understanding with every nation and to avoid by every honorable means the calamities of war; and we shall best attain object by frankness and sincerity in our foreign intercourse, by prompt and faithful execution of treaties, and by justice and equality in our conduct to all. But no nation, however desirous of peace, can hope to escape occasional collisions with other powers; and soundest dictates of policy require that we should place a condition to assert our rights if a resort to force should be necessary. Our local situation, our long line of seacoast, numerous bays, with deep rivers opening into the interior, as our extended and still increasing commerce, point to the natural means of defense. It will, in the end, be found to be the cheapest and most effectual; and now is the time, in a season of peace, and with an overflowing revenue, that we can, year after year, add to its strength without increasing the burdens of the people. It is your true policy. For your navy will not only protect your rich and flourishing commerce in distant seas, but will enable you to reach and annoy the enemy and will give to defense its greatest efficiency by meeting danger at a distance from home. It is impossible by any line of fortifications to guard every point from attack against a hostile force advancing from the ocean and selecting its object; but they are indispensable to protect cities from bombardment, dock yards and naval arsenals from destruction; to give shelter to merchant vessels in time of war, and to single ships or weaker squadrons when pressed by superior force. Fortifications of this description cannot be too soon completed and armed and placed in a condition of the most perfect preparation. The abundant means we now possess cannot be applied in any manner more useful to the country; and when this is done and our naval force sufficiently strengthened and our militia armed, we need not fear that any nation will wantonly insult us or needlessly provoke hostilities. We shall more certainly preserve peace when it is well understood that we are prepared for war.

CONCLUSION

In presenting to you, my fellow citizens, these parting counsels, I have

Jackson medal depicting the Battle of New Orleans. The Battle of Plattsburgh Bay, New York, occurred on Christmas Eve 1814. It was the last armed clash of the War of 1812 before the Treaty of Ghent officially ended hostilities. But it was not the last battle. The United States won a stunning victory at New Orleans in January 1815 under the command of General Andrew Jackson. This took place two weeks after the Treaty of Ghent had been signed, but more than a month before news of the treaty reached America. Jackson became the Hero of New Orleans, the nation's most prominent person since George Washington.

brought before you the leading principles upon which I endeavored to administer the Government in the high office with which you twice honored me. Knowing that the path of freedom is continually beset by enemies who often assume the disguise of friends, I have devoted the last hours of my public life to warn you of the danger. The progress of the United States under our free and happy institutions has surpassed the most sanguine hopes of the founders of the Republic. Our growth has been rapid beyond all former example, in numbers, in wealth, in knowledge, and all the useful arts which contribute to the comforts and convenience of man; and from the earliest ages of history to the present day, there never have been thirteen millions of people associated together in one political body who enjoyed so much freedom and happiness as the people of these United States. You have no longer any cause to fear danger from abroad; your strength and power are well known throughout the civilized world, as well as the high and gallant bearing of your sons. It is from within, among yourselves, from cupidity, from corruption, from disappointed ambition, and inordinate thirst for power, that factions will be formed and liberty endangered. It is against such designs, whatever disguise the actors may assume, that you have especially to guard yourselves. You have the highest of human trust committed to your care. Providence has showered on this favored land blessings without number and has chosen you as the guardian of freedom to preserve it for the benefit of the human race. May He who holds in his hands the destinies of nations make you worthy of the favors He has bestowed and enable you, with pure hearts and pure hands and sleepless vigilance, to guard and defend to to the end of time the great charge he has committed to your keeping.

My own race is nearly run; advanced age and failing health warn me that before long I must pass beyond the reach of human event and cease to feel the vicissitudes of human affairs. I thank God that my life has been spent in a land of liberty and that He has given me a heart to love my country with the affection of a son. And, filled with gratitude for your constant and unwavering kindness, I bid you a last and affectionate farewell.

Further READING

GENERAL REFERENCE

Israel, Fred L. *Student's Atlas of American Presidential Elections, 1789–1996*. Washington, D.C.: Congressional Quarterly Books, 1998.

Levy, Peter B., editor. *100 Key Documents in American History*. Westport, Conn.: Praeger, 1999.

Mieczkowski, Yarek. *The Routledge Historical Atlas of Presidential Elections*. New York: Routledge, 2001.

Polsby, Nelson W., and Aaron Wildavsky. *Presidential Elections: Strategies and Structures of American Politics*. 10th edition. New York: Chatham House, 2000.

Watts, J. F., and Fred L. Israel, editors. *Presidential Documents*. New York: Routledge, 2000.

Widmer, Ted. *The New York Times Campaigns: A Century of Presidential Races*. New York: DK Publishing, 2000.

POLITICAL AMERICANA REFERENCE

Cunningham, Noble E. Jr. *Popular Images of the Presidency: From Washington to Lincoln*. Columbia: University of Missouri Press, 1991.

Melder, Keith. *Hail to the Candidate: Presidential Campaigns from Banners to Broadcasts*. Washington, D.C.: Smithsonian Institution Press, 1992.

Schlesinger, Arthur M. jr., Fred L. Israel, and David J. Frent. *Running for President: The Candidates and their Images*. 2 vols. New York: Simon and Schuster, 1994.

Warda, Mark. *100 Years of Political Campaign Collectibles*. Clearwater, Fla.: Galt Press, 1996.

THE ELECTION OF 1828
and the Administration of Andrew Jackson

Booraem, Hendrick. *Young Hickory: The Making of Andrew Jackson*. San Diego: Taylor Publishing, 2001.

Brookhiser, Richard. *America's First Dynasty: The Adamses, 1735–1918*. New York: Free Press, 2002.

Harmon, Daniel E. *Andrew Jackson*. Philadelphia: Mason Crest Publishers, 2003.

Meltzer, Milton. *Andrew Jackson and His America*. New York: Franklin Watts, 1993.

Nagel, Paul C. *John Quincy Adams: A Public Life, A Private Life*. New York: Alfred Knopf, 1997.

Niven, John. *Martin Van Buren: The Romantic Age of American Politics*. New York: American Political Biography Press, 2000

Remini, Robert V. *Henry Clay: Statesman for the Union*. New York: W. W. Norton, 1991.

———. *The Life of Andrew Jackson*. New York: Harper Perennial, 2001.

Schlesinger, Arthur M. jr., *The Age of Jackson*. Boston: Little, Brown, 1945.

Silbey, Joel, ed. *The American Party Battle: Election Campaign Battles, 1828–1876*. Cambridge, Mass.: The Harvard University Press, 1999.

A

Adams, Charles Francis, 30
Adams, John Quincy, 8–9, 17, 19, 26, 29, 31, ***39***, ***73***
  libelous charges against, 29–30
  memorabilia, ***18***, ***21***, ***23***, ***24***, ***29***, ***33***, ***43***, ***44***, ***95***
Alamo, 38
Ambrister, Robert, 35
American (New York), 32
American System, 27
  See also Clay, Henry
Annual Message, 12
Arbuthnot, Alexander, 35
Argus (Albany), 29
Argus of Western America (Kentucky), 29

B

Baltimore, Maryland, 22
Bank War, 10
banking policy, 100–102
Battle of New Orleans, 20, 21, 25, ***104***
Battle of Plattsburgh Bay, ***104***
Benton, Thomas Hart, 18
Binns, John, 34–35
Boston, Massachusetts, 30, ***44***
Brown's Indian Queen Hotel, 50
Burr, Aaron, 35
Burr Conspiracy, 35

C

Calhoun, John C., 18, 36, 68, ***73***
campaigning, 8–14, 30–31, 35
  in 1828, 17, 20–26, 30, 32–33
  "front porch," 11
  literature, ***28***, ***56***, ***73***, ***84–85***, ***101***
Charleston, South Carolina, 71
Cherokees. *See* Native Americans
Chesapeake and Ohio Canal, 38, 88–89
Clay, Henry, 17, 18, 21, 26, 27, 30, 32, 82, ***84***
"Coffin Hand Bill," 34–35, ***84–85***
  See also press
Congress
  powers of, 64–67, 68, 70, 78
  See also House of Representatives
Constitution, United States, 41, 42, 59, 63, 64–65, 93–94
    and the electoral system, 17
    and executive powers, 52, 55
    and federal powers, 55–57, 98–99
    and interstate commerce, 88–89
    and judicial powers, 76
    and Nullification, 69–81
    and political parties, 6–8
    separation of powers, 7–8
Constitutional Whig (Virginia), 32
Courier (New York), 29
Crawford, William H., 17
Creek War, 34, ***84–85***
currency, 100–102

Numbers in ***bold italics*** refer to captions.

D

debt, national, 38, 42, ***84***
defense, national, 42, 44, 102–103
Democratic Party, 17, 18–20, 22, 35, 50, ***84***
  campaigning, 25, 26, 30
  and the press, 31–32
  See also parties, political
Democratic Press (Philadelphia), 34–35

E

election, presidential, 45
  of 1824, 17, ***22***, 30, ***39***
  of 1832, 58, 82
  of 1876, ***24***
  and the 1828 campaign, 17, ***27***, 35, ***56***
  and campaigning, 8–14
  electoral votes, ***39***
  process of, 6, 15
electoral system, 17, ***22***, ***39***
Enquirer (Richmond), 29
ethnicity, 27, 29
Evening Post (New York), 29
executive powers
  limits of, 41, 45, 98–99
  vetoing, 52
  See also government, Federal

F

farewell address, Andrew Jackson's, 90–105
  See also speeches
First Seminole War, 35
Florida (territory), 35
foreign policy, 83, 93, 102–103
Founding Fathers
  and political parties, 6–7, 8–9
"front porch" campaigning, 11
  See also campaigning

G

Gazette (Cincinnati), 32–34
Gazette (Illinois), 32
Georgia, 17
Godfrey, Martha, 30
government, Federal
  and the Constitution, 55–57, 66
  and exclusive privileges, 64
  powers of, 98–99
  and the Second Bank, 60–61

H

Hammond, Charles, 32–34
Hill, Isaac, 30
House of Representatives
  and the election of 1824, 17
  John Quincy Adams in the, ***43***
  See also Congress

I

inaugural address
  Andrew Jackson's first, 40–42, 44–45
  Andrew Jackson's second, 82–84, 86–87
  See also speeches
Indian Removal Act of 1830, 38, 46–49, 92–93
  See also Native Americans
Inquirer (New York), 29

J

Jackson, Andrew ("Old Hickory"), 9, 10, ***19***, ***20***, ***73***, ***84–85***
  in the 1824 election, 17
  cabinet of, 37
  campaigning of, 18–19, 22–26, 35
  and the Chesapeake and Ohio Canal strike, 88–89
  facts at a glance, 36–39
  farewell speech of, 90–105
  and the federal Union, 71–81, 83–84, 86–87, 93–97
  and foreign policy, 83, 93, 102–103
  inaugural address (first), 40–42, 44–45
  inaugural address (second), 82–84, 86–87
  and the Indian Removal Act of 1830, 46–49
  marriage of, to Rachel Donelson Robards, 32–33
  memorabilia, ***18***, 20–21, ***22***, ***27***, ***32***, ***34***, ***37***, ***48***, ***56***, ***63***, ***95***, ***101***, ***104***
  and Native Americans, 44–45, 46–49, 92–93
  and Nullification, 68–81, 97–98
  political offices of, 37

popularity of, 20–21, 24–25
and the press, 32–35
reelection of, 38
vetoes the Maysville Road Bill, 52–57
vetoes the Second Bank, 58–67
Volunteer Toast of, 50–51
Jackson, Rachel Donelson Robards (Mrs. Andrew Jackson), 32–33, 36, 40
Jefferson, Thomas, 17
Jefferson Day Dinner, 50
Journal (Massachusetts), 32

K

Kentucky, 17, 52

L

labor strike (at the Chesapeake and Ohio Canal), 38, 88–89
Lafayette, Marquis de, ***35***
literature, campaign, ***28***, ***56***, ***73***, ***84–85***, ***101***
Louisiana Central Committee, 23
Love Laughs at Locksmiths, 25
Ludlow, Noah M., 35

M

Madison, James, 17
Massachusetts, 17, ***28***, ***43***
Maysville Road Bill of 1830, 52–57
media, role of
in elections, 12–13
See also press
memorabilia, political, ***31***, ***35***
Andrew Jackson, ***18***, 20–21, ***22***, ***27***, ***32***, ***34***, ***37***, ***48***, ***56***, ***63***, ***95***, ***101***, ***104***
John Quincy Adams, ***18***, ***21***, ***23***, ***24***, ***29***, ***33***, ***43***, ***44***, ***95***
Mercury (Charleston), 29
Mississippi River, 23, 47, ***48***

N

Nashville, Tennessee, 19, 36
Nashville Central Committee, 32–33
National Intelligencer (Washington, D.C.), 31
National Journal (Washington, D.C.), 31
National Republican Party, 17, 18, 21, 26, 82, ***84***
campaigning, 30
and the press, 31–32
See also parties, political
Native Americans
and Andrew Jackson, 44–45, 92–93
Indian Removal Act of 1830, 38, 46–49
New Hampshire, 30
New Orleans, Louisiana, 20, 23, ***104***
newspapers. *See* press
Niles Weekly Register (Baltimore), 32
Nullification, 38, 50, 68–81, 97–98

O

Ohio, 22
Ohio River, 55
"Old Hickory." *See* Jackson, Andrew

P

Pakenham, Sir Michael, 25
parties, political
and campaigning, 11–13, 17, 19–20
growth of, 6–9, 18
platforms of, 9, 10
Pennsylvania, 71
platforms, political party, 9, 10
President, United States
role of, 6–7, 13–14
presidential election. *See* election, presidential
press
role of, in the 1828 election, 29–30, 31–33

R

religion, 27, 29
Reporter (Kentucky), 32
Republican (Missouri), 32
Revolution, American, 21
Robards, Lewis, 32
Robards, Rachel Donelson (Mrs. Andrew Jackson), 32–33, 36, 40
Roberts, Lewis. *See* Robards, Lewis

S

secede, right to, 76–77, 79–80
Second Bank of the United States, 38, ***74***
President Jackson vetoes the, 58–67
slavery, ***95***
South Carolina, 38

and Nullification, 68–81
Specie Circular, 38
speeches, 11, 14
farewell address (Andrew Jackson), 90–105
first inaugural address (Andrew Jackson), 40–42, 44–45
second inaugural address (Andrew Jackson), 82–84, 86–87
State of the Union address. *See* Annual Message
states' rights, 41, 50–51, 53–54, 59, 62, 66–67, 77–78, 83–84, 86, 97–98
Statesman (Boston), 29
Supreme Court, United States, 63, 66, 69, ***73***

T

tariffs, 38, ***84***
and Nullification, 68–69
taxation, 71, 74, 99
Tennessee, 17, 38, 40
Texas, Republic of, 38
"Trail of Tears." *See* Indian Removal Act of 1830
Treaty of Ghent, ***104***

U

union, Federal, 50–51, 71–81, 83–84, 86–87, 93–97
United States Telegraph (Washington, D.C.), 29

V

Van Buren, Martin, 9–10, 18–19, 36, 37
Virginia, 71
Volunteer Toast, Jackson's, 50–51

W

War of 1812, 8, 20, 21, 22, 23, 25, ***31***, ***35***, ***104***
Washington, D.C., 40, 50
Washington, George, 14, ***20***, 94, 95, ***104***
and political parties, 7
Waxhaw, South Carolina, ***32***, 36
Webster, Daniel, 10, 14, 18, 30
Whig Party, 9, 10, 38, ***84***
See also parties, political
Williamsport, Maryland, 88
Woodworth, Samuel, 25

Arthur M. Schlesinger Jr. holds the Albert Schweitzer Chair in the Humanities at the Graduate Center of the City University of New York. He is the author of more than a dozen books, including *The Age of Jackson*; *The Vital Center; The Age of Roosevelt* (3 vols.); *A Thousand Days: John F. Kennedy in the White House; Robert Kennedy and His Times; The Cycles of American History;* and *The Imperial Presidency.* Professor Schlesinger served as Special Assistant to President Kennedy (1961–63). His numerous awards include: the Pulitzer Prize for History; the Pulitzer Prize for Biography; two National Book Awards; The Bancroft Prize; and the American Academy of Arts and Letters Gold Medal for History.

Fred L. Israel is professor emeritus of American history, City College of New York. He is the author of *Nevada's Key Pittman* and has edited *The War Diary of Breckinridge Long* and *Major Peace Treaties of Modern History, 1648–1975* (5 vols.) He holds the Scribe's Award from the American Bar Association for his joint editorship of the *Justices of the United States Supreme Court* (4 vols.). For more than 25 years Professor Israel has compiled and edited the Gallup Poll into annual reference volumes.

David J. Frent is the president of Political Americana Auctions, Oakhurst, NJ. With his wife, Janice, he has assembled the nation's foremost private collection of political campaign memorabilia. Mr. Frent has designed exhibits for corporations, the Smithsonian Institution, and the United States Information Agency. A member of the board of directors of the American Political Items Collectors since 1972, he was elected to its Hall of Fame for his "outstanding contribution to preserving and studying our political heritage."